Configuring Product Information Management Within Dynamics AX 2012

BY MURRAY FIFE

ISBN-10: 151170148X

ISBN-13: 978-1511701488

© 2015 Blind Squirrel Publishing, LLC, All Rights
www.dynamicsaxcompanions.com

Preface

What You Need For This Guide

All the examples shown in this blueprint were done with the Microsoft Dynamics AX 2012 virtual machine image that was downloaded from the Microsoft CustomerSource or PartnerSource site. If you don't have your own installation of Microsoft Dynamics AX 2012, you can also use the images found on the Microsoft Learning Download Center or deployed through Lifecycle Services. The following list of software from the virtual image was leveraged within this guide:

• Microsoft Dynamics AX 2012 R3

Even though all the preceding software was used during the development and testing of the recipes in this book, they may also work on earlier versions of the software with minor tweaks and adjustments, and should also work on later versions without any changes.

Errata

Although we have taken every care to ensure the accuracy of our content, mistakes do happen. If you find a mistake in one of our books—maybe a mistake in the text or the code—we would be grateful if you would report this to us. By doing so, you can save other readers from frustration and help us improve subsequent versions of this book. If you find any errata, please report them by emailing editor@dynamicsaxcompanions.com.

Piracy

Piracy of copyright material on the Internet is an ongoing problem across all media. If you come across any illegal copies of our works, in any form, on the Internet, please provide us with the location address or website name immediately so that we can pursue a remedy.

Please contact us at legal@dynamicsaxcompanions.com with a link to the suspected pirated material.

We appreciate your help in protecting our authors, and our ability to bring you valuable content.

Questions

You can contact us at help@dynamicsaxcompanions.com if you are having a problem with any aspect of the book, and we will do our best to address it.

Table Of Contents

CONFIGURING DIMENSIONAL PRODUCTS (Ctd)

INTRODUCTION

The Product Information Management area within Dynamics AX not only allows you to manage all of the core product details. It is also the central location for all the other product information such as the Product Attributes, Product Categories, External Product Descriptions and Product Structures. It also allows you to track the interrelationships between the products through this part of the system with the Product Relationships. If you want to add more control over the products lifecycle then you can use the Product Change Management Cases. All of this information is managed through this one location and then consumed within all of the other modules.

Setting up the Product and Service details are not hard either and this guide is designed to give you step by step instructions to show you how to configure the Product Information Management area, and also how some of the basic parts work to get you up and running and working with your Products and Services.

CONFIGURING PRODUCT INFORMATION MANAGEMENT CONTROLS

Before we start creating products within the Product Information Management area of Dynamics AX, there are a couple of codes that need to configured so that everything will run smoothly. In this section we will walk through everything that you need to set up to get the basic Product Information Management features working.

Configuring Storage Dimension Groups

First we will need to set up we need to set up the **Storage Dimension Groups**. These allow you to control the level to which you track the location of the products.

Configuring Storage Dimension Groups

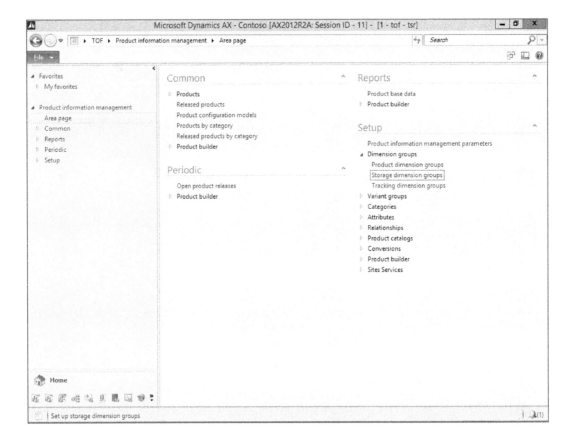

To do this, click on the **Storage Dimension Groups** menu item within the **Dimension Groups** folder of the **Setup** group within the **Product Information Management** area page.

Configuring Storage Dimension Groups

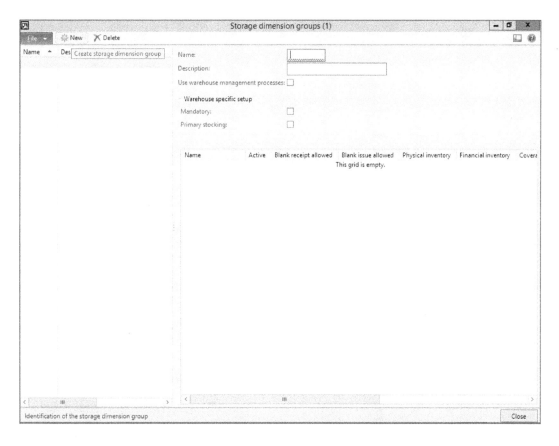

When the **Storage Dimension Groups** maintenance form is displayed, click on the **New** button in the menu bar to create a new record.

Configuring Storage Dimension Groups

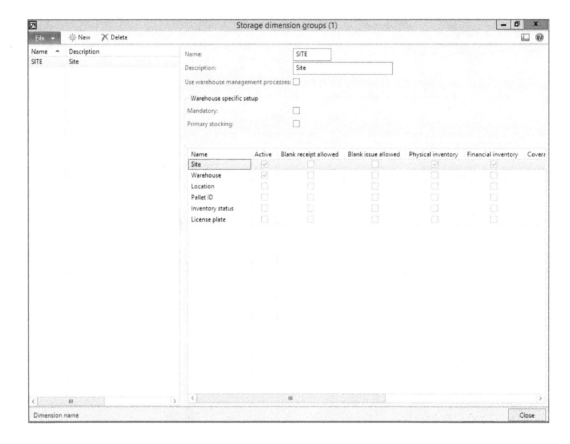

The first record that we will create will be to track the inventory at the site level only. So set the **Name** to **SITE** and the **Description** to **Site**.

You will notice that the storage dimension levels will be populated with different flags to manage how you track the storage locations.

Configuring Storage Dimension Groups

If you scroll over to the right you will see even more options are available.

Configuring Storage Dimension Groups

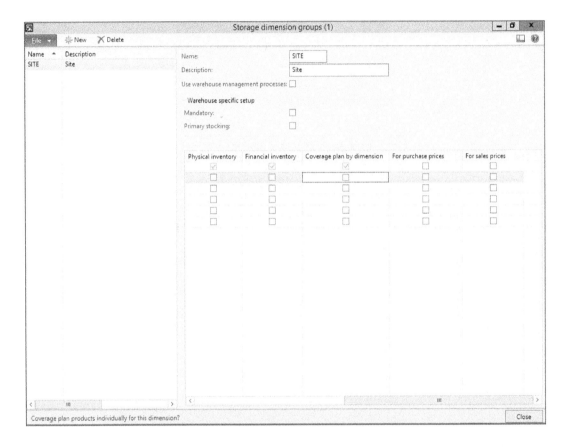

For this storage dimension, uncheck the **Coverage Plan By Dimension** flag at the warehouse level to make this only tracked at the site level.

Configuring Storage Dimension Groups

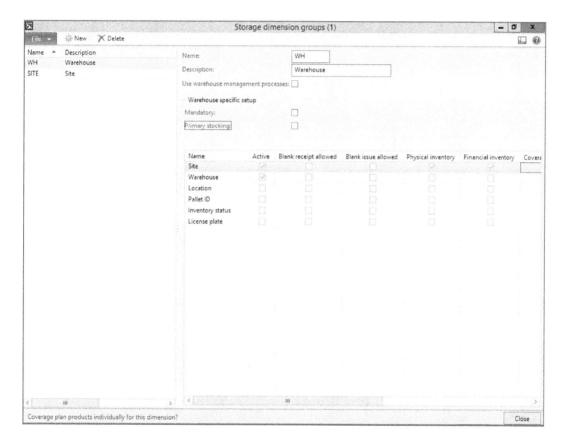

Next we will want to create a storage dimension that allows us to track the inventory at the warehouse level. To do this, click on the **New** button in the menu bar to create a new record and then set the **Name** to **WH** and the **Description** to **Warehouse**.

Configuring Storage Dimension Groups

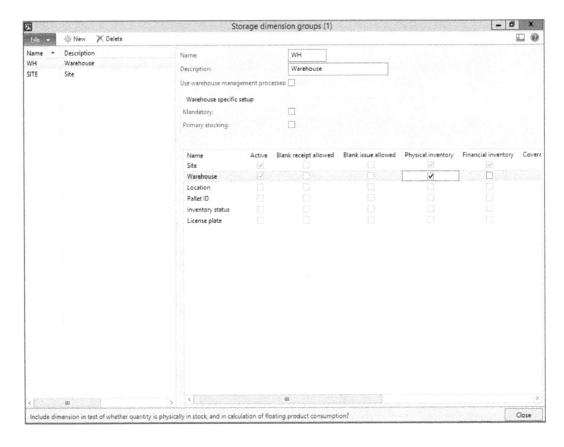

Check the **Physical Inventory** flag for the **Warehouse** level.

Configuring Storage Dimension Groups

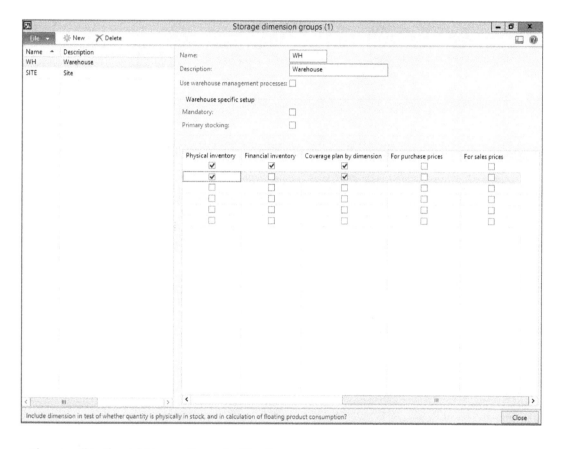

Then scroll to the right to see the rest of the flags.

Configuring Storage Dimension Groups

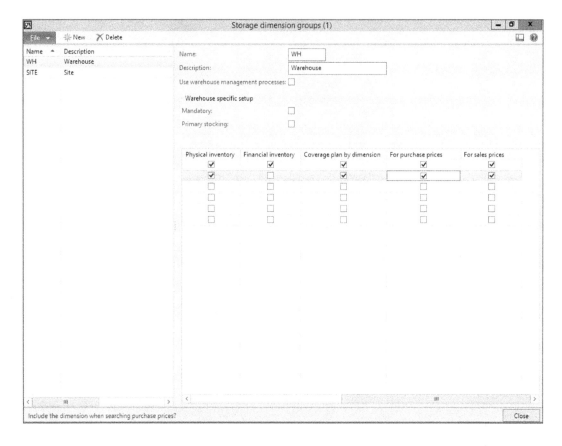

This will allow you to check the **For Purchase Prices** and **For Sales Prices** flags against the **Warehouse** as well.

Configuring Storage Dimension Groups

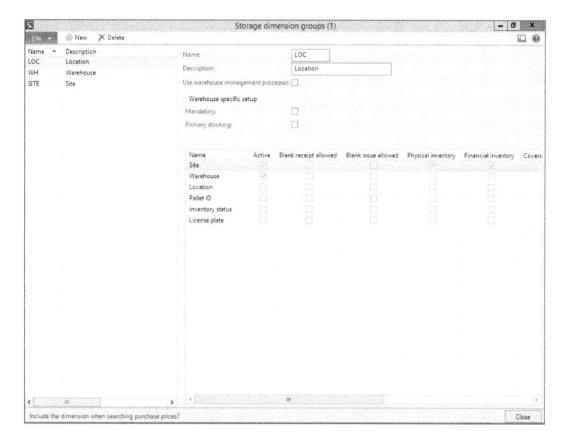

Finally we will want to create a storage dimension that allows us to track the inventory at the down to the inventory location level. To do this, click on the **New** button in the menu bar to create a new record and then set the **Name** to **LOC** and the **Description** to **Location**.

Configuring Storage Dimension Groups

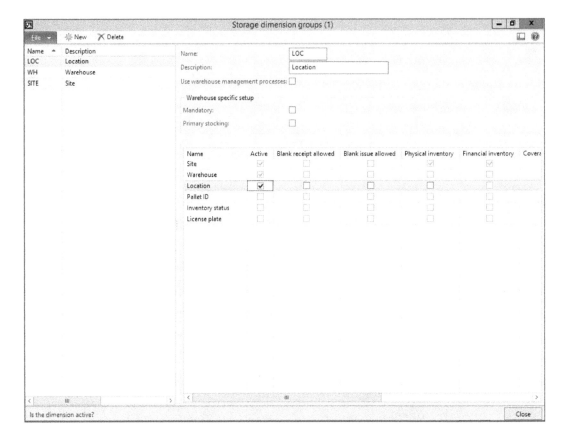

For this record, check the **Active** flag for the **Location** inventory level.

Configuring Storage Dimension Groups

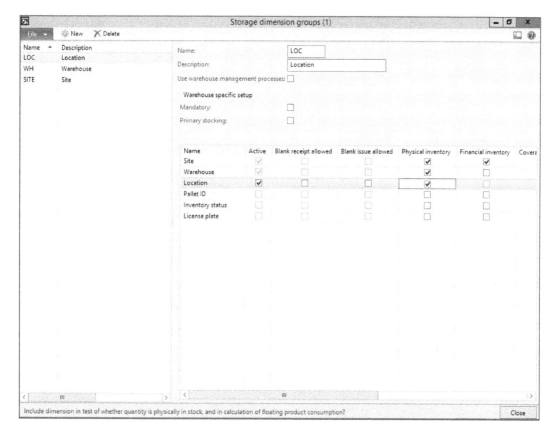

Then check the **Physical Inventory** flags for both the **Warehouse** and the **Location**.

Configuring Storage Dimension Groups

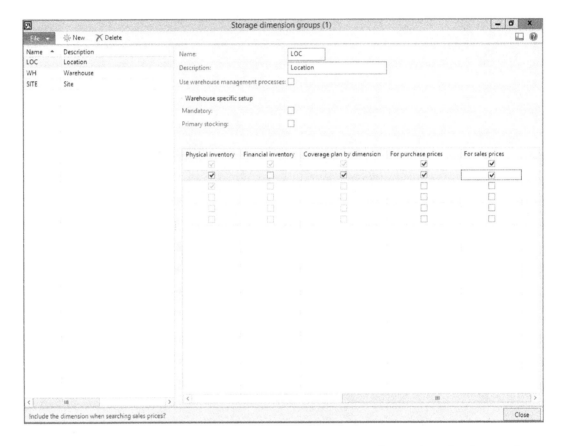

Then scroll over to the right and check the **For Purchase Prices** and **For Sales Prices** flags at the **Warehouse** level.

Note: We don't want to check the prices for the **Location** level because that would make us track different costs for each warehouse location.

When you have done that, click on the **Close** button to exit from the form.

Configuring Product Tracking Dimensions

Next we need to set up the **Product Tracking Dimensions** which are used to identify if products are going to be Batch and/or Serial Number controlled.

Configuring Product Tracking Dimensions

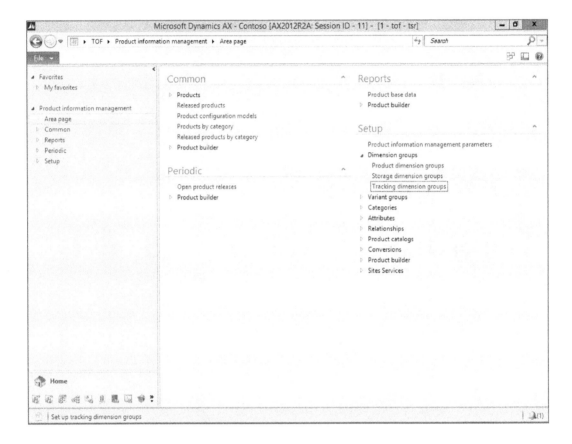

To do this, click on the **Tracking Dimension Groups** menu item within the **Dimension Groups** folder of the **Setup** group within the **Product Information Management** area page.

Configuring Product Tracking Dimensions

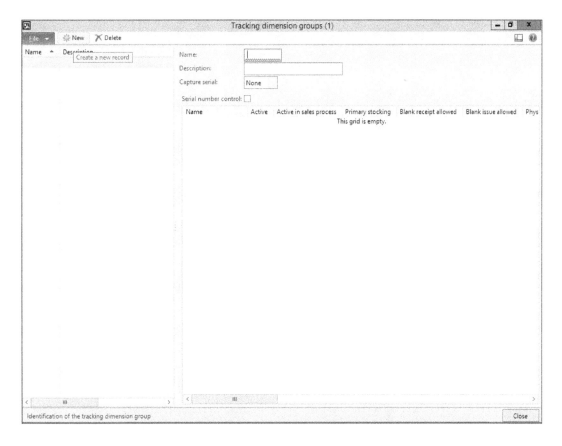

When the **Tracking Dimensions** maintenance form is displayed, click on the **New** button in the menu bar to create a new record.

Configuring Product Tracking Dimensions

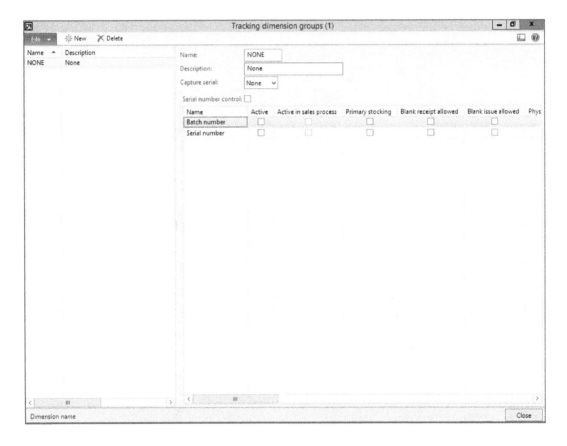

The first **Tracking Dimension** that we will create will be to track nothing, which we can use for products that we don't care if they get intermingled. So set the **Name** to **NONE** and the **Description** to None.

Configuring Product Tracking Dimensions

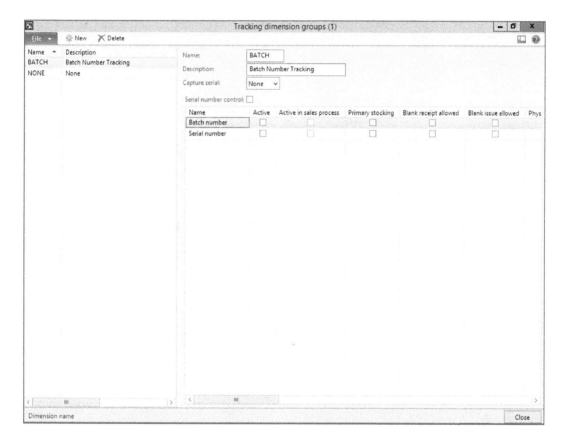

The next **Tracking Dimension** that we will create will be to track batch or lot controlled items. To do this, click on the **New** button in the menu bar and then set the **Name** to **BATCH** and the **Description** to **Batch Number Tracking**.

Configuring Product Tracking Dimensions

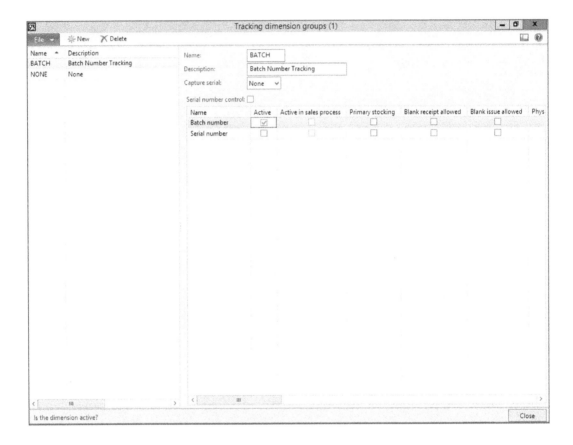

Then set the **Active** flag for the **Batch Number** tracking level.

Configuring Product Tracking Dimensions

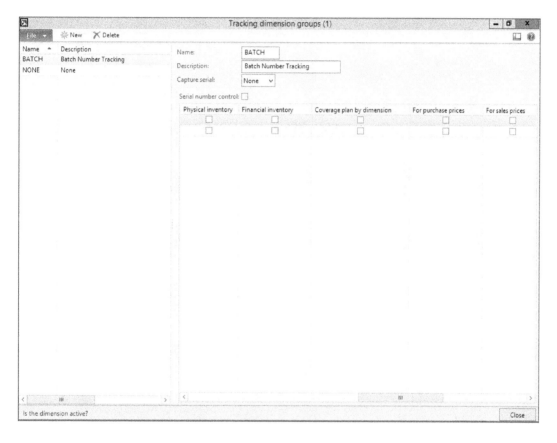

Then scroll over to the right and you will see that there are some more flags that are available to set against the tracking dimensions.

Configuring Product Tracking Dimensions

Then set the **Physical Inventory** flag at the **Batch Number** tracking dimension.

Configuring Product Tracking Dimensions

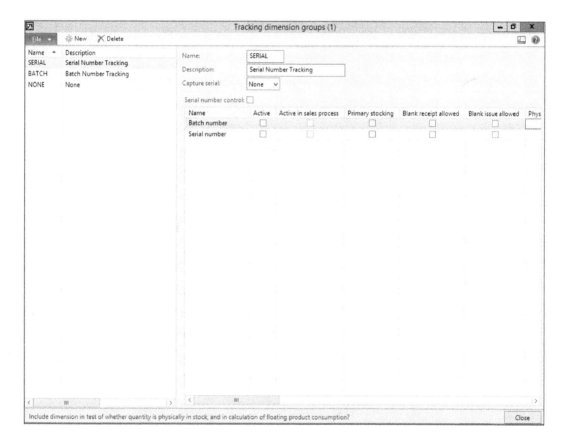

Now we will create **Tracking Dimension** that tracks the serial numbers against items. To do this, click on the **New** button in the menu bar and then set the **Name** to **SERIAL** and the **Description** to **Serial Number Tracking**.

Configuring Product Tracking Dimensions

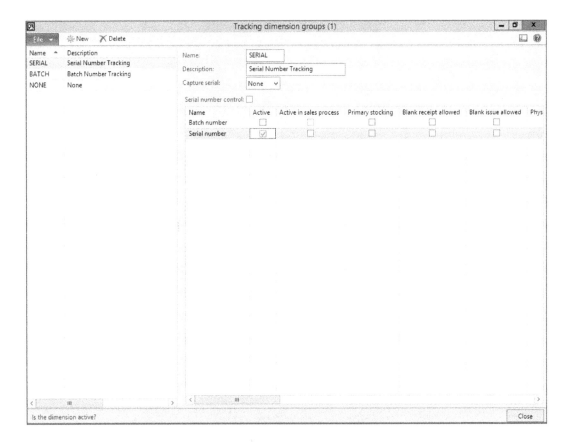

Then set the **Active** flag for the **Serial Number** tracking level.

Configuring Product Tracking Dimensions

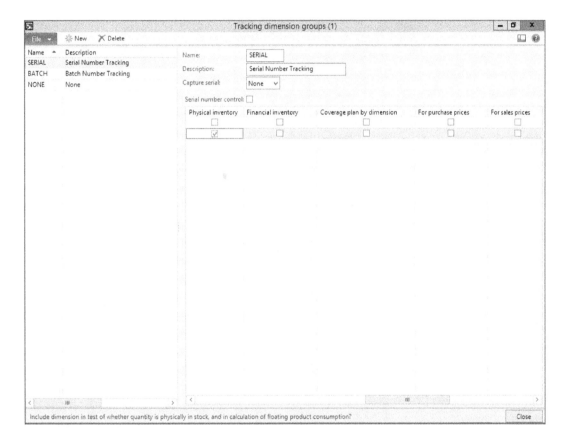

Scroll over to the right on the tracking dimension flags and set the **Physical Inventory** flag at the **Serial Number** tracking dimension.

Configuring Product Tracking Dimensions

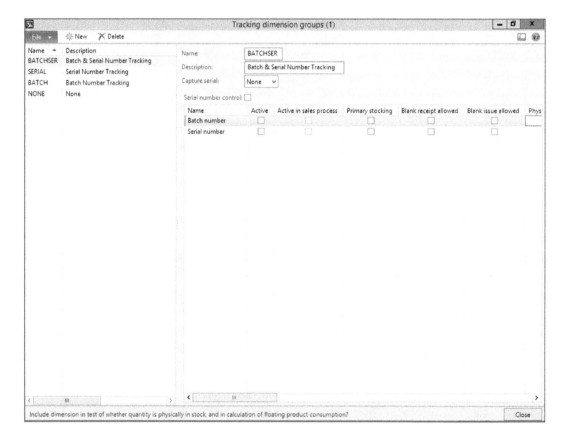

Finally we will create **Tracking Dimension** that tracks the both the batch and serial numbers against items. To do this, click on the **New** button in the menu bar and then set the **Name** to **BATCHSER** and the **Description** to **Batch & Serial Number Tracking**.

Configuring Product Tracking Dimensions

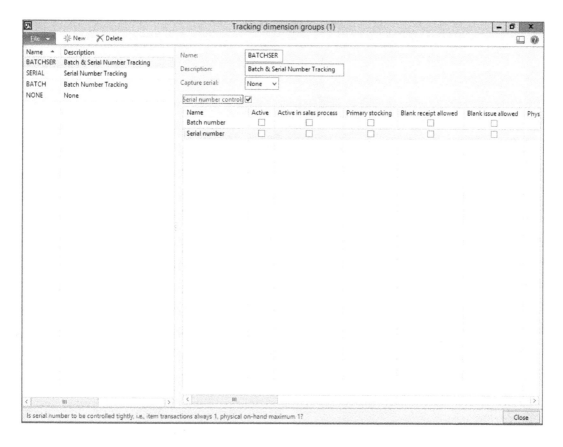

Also for this tracking dimension, check the **Serial Number Control** flag.

Configuring Product Tracking Dimensions

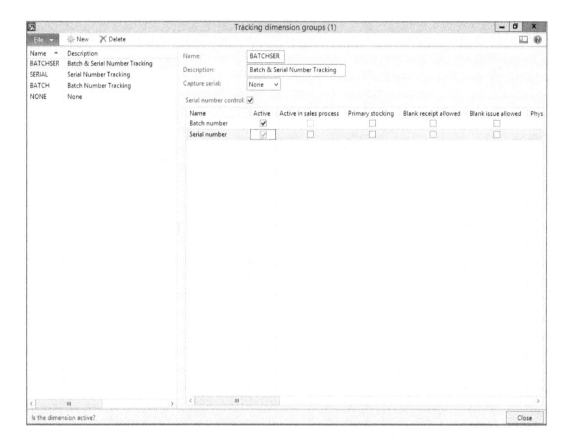

Then set the **Active** flag for both the **Batch Number** and the **Serial Number** tracking levels.

Configuring Product Tracking Dimensions

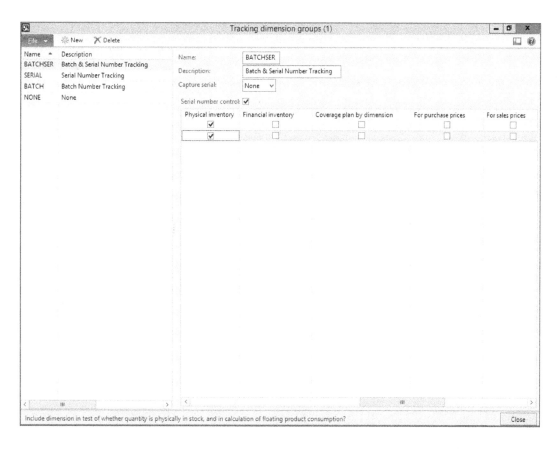

Then scroll over to the right on the tracking dimension flags and set the **Physical Inventory** flag on the **Batch Number** and **Serial Number** tracking dimension.

Adding New Units Of Measure

Although Dynamics AX is preconfigured with a whole slew of default **Units of Measures**, there will probably be some additional ones that are specific to our products that are not part of the standard data. So before we start setting up our products, we will want to quickly set up a few more **Units Of Measures**.

Adding New Units Of Measure

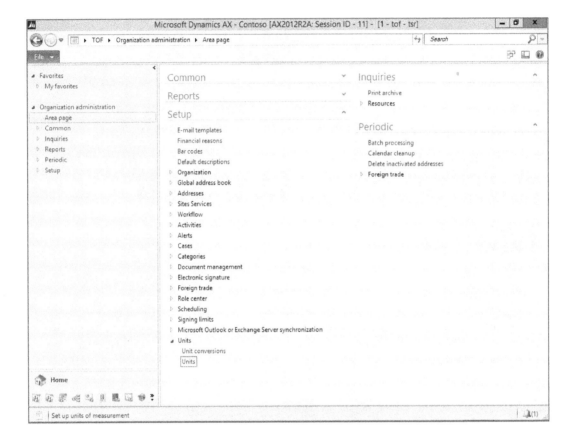

To do this, click on the **Units** menu item within the **Units** folder of the **Setup** group within the **Organization Administration** area page.

Adding New Units Of Measure

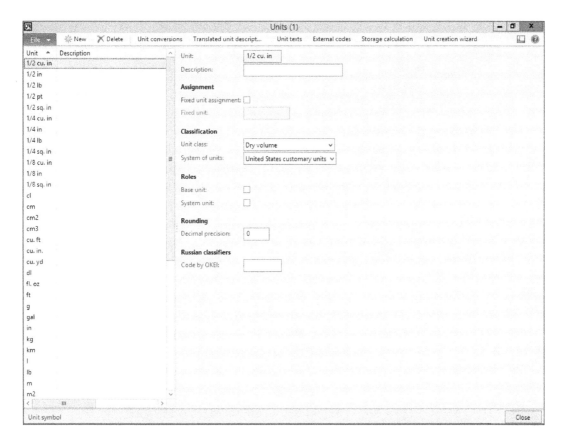

When the **Units** maintenance form is displayed you will see that there are already a lot of **Unites Of Measure** that are loaded into the base system.

Adding New Units Of Measure

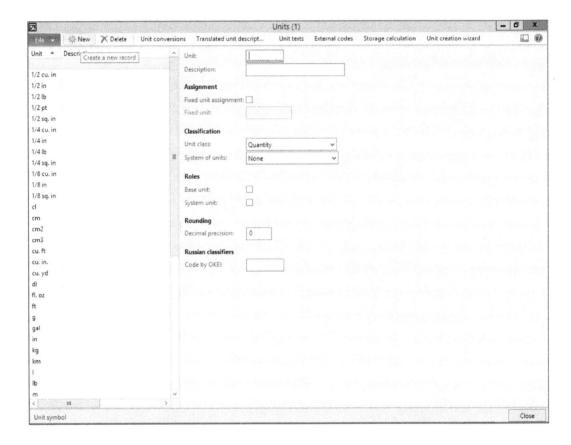

Click on the **New** button within the menu bar to create a new record.

Adding New Units Of Measure

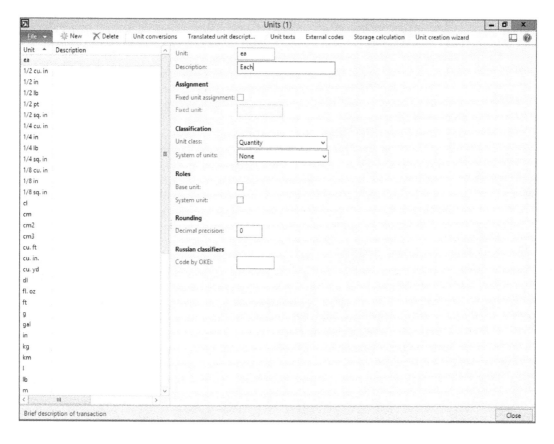

For the first unit of measure we will configure an **Each** unit. So set the **Unit** to **ea** and the **Description** to **Each**.

Adding New Units Of Measure

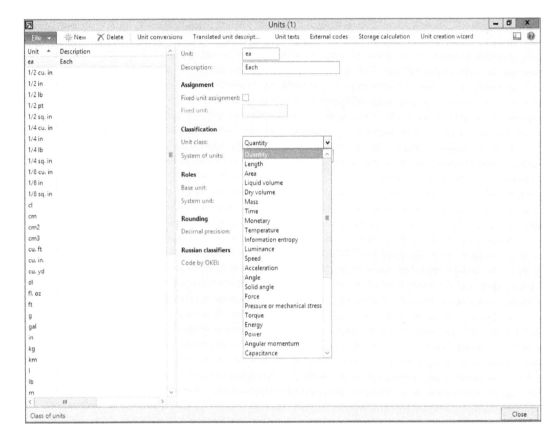

If you click on the **Unit Class** you will be able to see that there are a number of different classifications that you can assign to your **Unit**. Select the **Quantity Unit Class** for this record.

Note: Selecting the **Unit Class** is important because when you want to perform Unit Of Measure Conversions, then you will be asked if you want to convert within the Unit Class or configure an Intra-Class conversion. It's tidier if all of the same common units are within the same Unit Class.

Adding New Units Of Measure

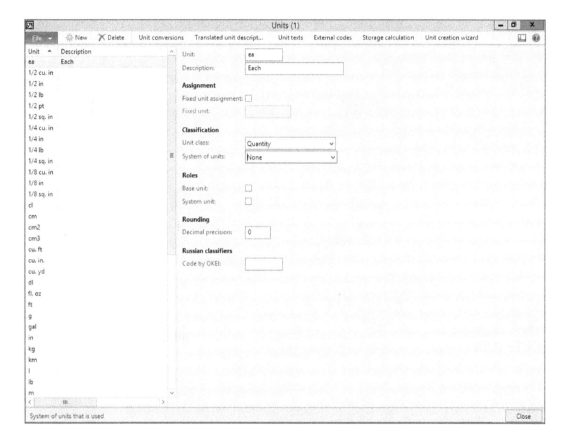

Once you have done that, your **Unit Of Measure** is configured.

Adding New Units Of Measure

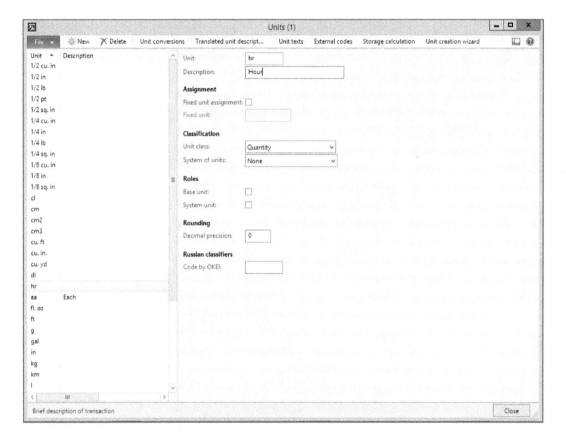

We will create a couple more **Units Of Measure** before we finish, so click on the **New** button in the menu bar to create a new record and set the **Unit** to **hr** and the **Description** to **Hour**.

Adding New Units Of Measure

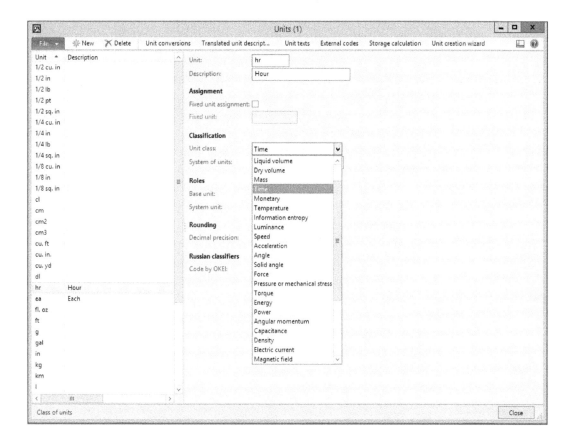

For this unit, click on the dropdown list for the **Unit Class** field and select the **Time** Unit Class.

Adding New Units Of Measure

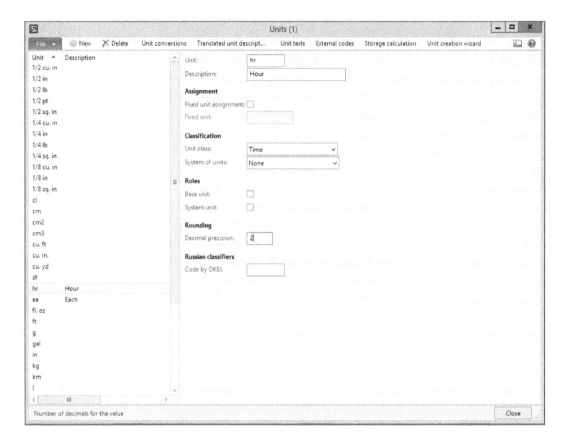

Also, change the **Decimal Precision** field within the **Rounding** field group to 2 so that we will round this number to two decimal places.

Adding New Units Of Measure

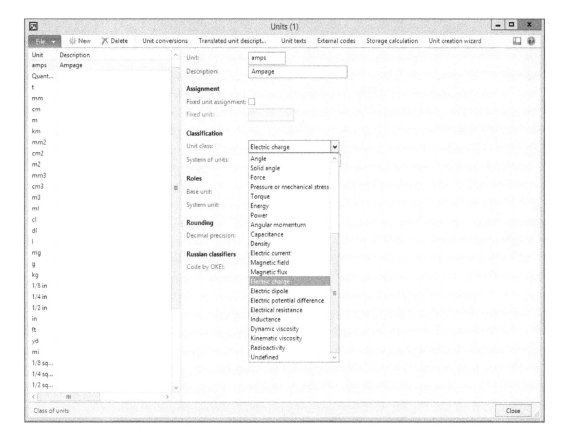

Now create one last **Units Of Measure**, by clicking on the **New** button in the menu bar to create a new record and setting the **Unit** to **amps** and **Description** to **Ampage**, and then selecting the **Electric Charge** from the **Unit Class** field dropdown.

Adding New Units Of Measure

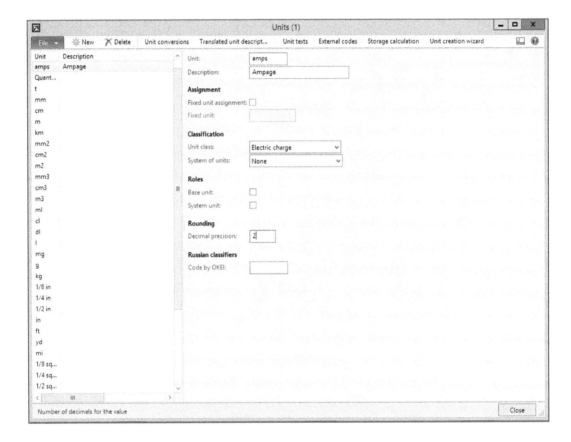

And then set the **Decimal Precision** to **2**.

Once you have done that, click on the **Close** button to exit from the form.

CONFIGURING PRODUCTS & SERVICES

Now that you have all of the basic codes and controls configured you can start adding some real products and services into the Product Information Management area.

In this chapter we will show you how you can set up products and services, and also how you can load in all of your products in bulk through the Data Import Export Framework.

Creating A Product

Now we can start creating our products. There are a number of different product types that you can configure based on if it is a physical product or a service item, if the product is a simple product or a includes additional configurations and dimensions, and even if the product is configurable based on rules.

In this first example we will start off by creating a simple inventoried item.

Creating A Product

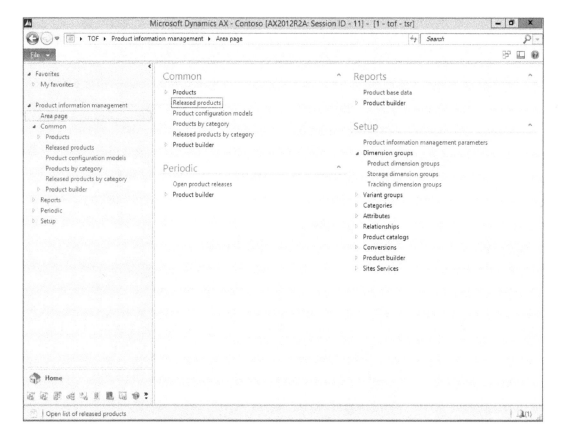

To do this, click on the **Released Products** menu item within the **Common** group of the **Product Information Management** area page.

Creating A Product

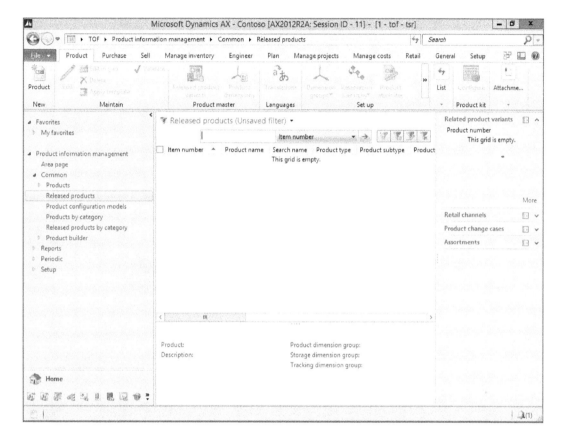

When the **Released Products** list page is displayed, click on the **Product** button within the **New** group of the **Product** ribbon bar.

Creating A Product

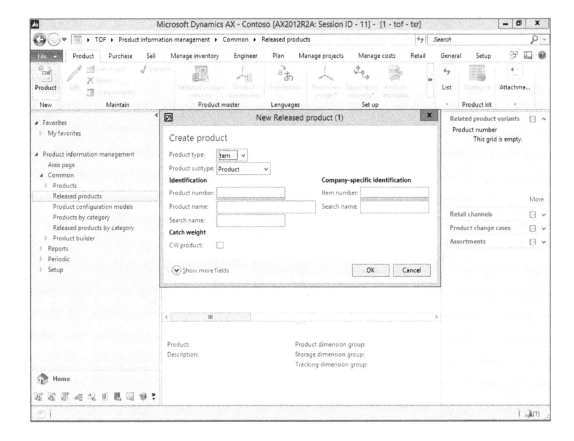

This will open up the **New Released Product** creation dialog box.

Creating A Product

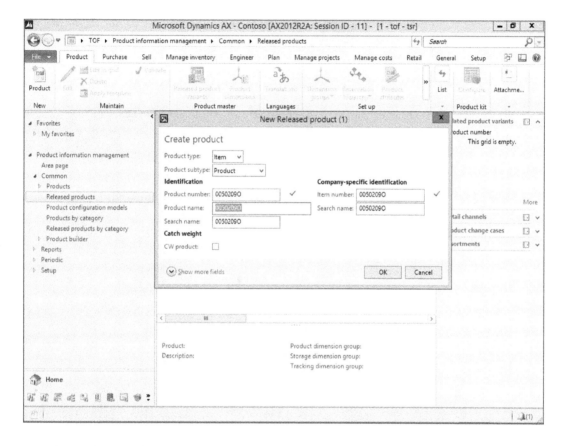

Set the **Product Number** to **0050209O**.

Creating A Product

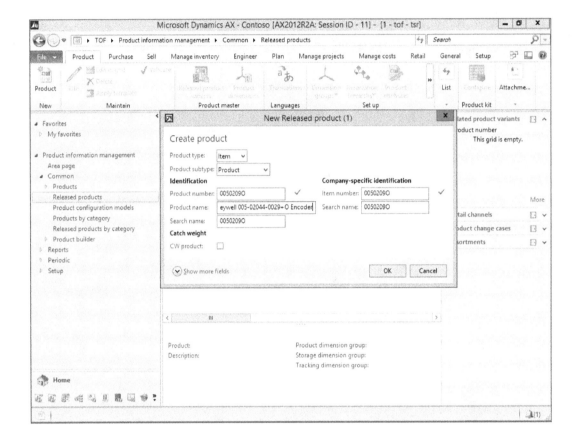

The **Product Name** will default in based off the **Product Number** so we will want to change it to something a little more descriptive like **Honeywell 005-02044-0029+O Encoder** or something shorter if you like.

Creating A Product

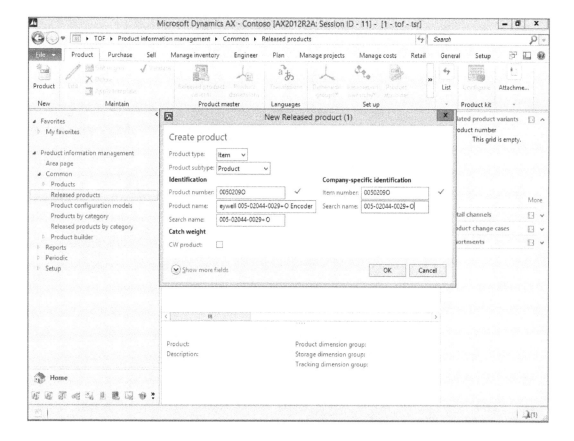

Next we will change both **Search Name** fields to **005-02044-0029+O**.

Note: There are two **Search Name** fields because you will really be setting up two product records when you do this. The first will be the global record and the second will be the one for the current company that you are in. Different organizations can have different part codes and descriptions that reference the same parent.

Now click on the **Show More Fields** button at the bottom of the form.

Creating A Product

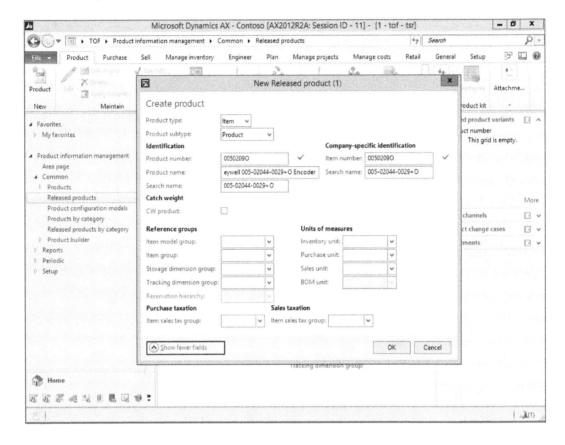

This will expand the form a little bit and show you some more fields that you can configure before you create the product.

Creating A Product

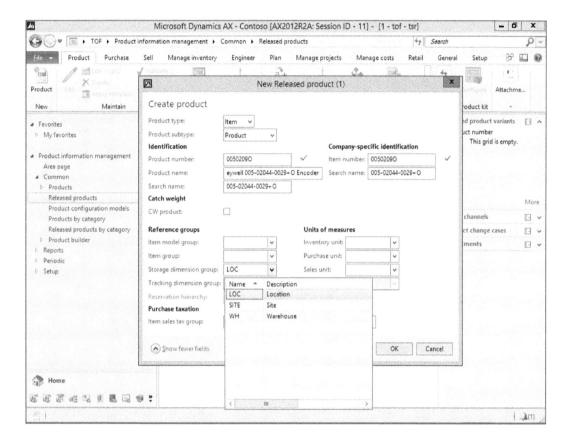

Click on the **Storage Dimension Group** field and select the **LOC** option that you configured earlier on so that we can track this product within our warehouse locations.

Creating A Product

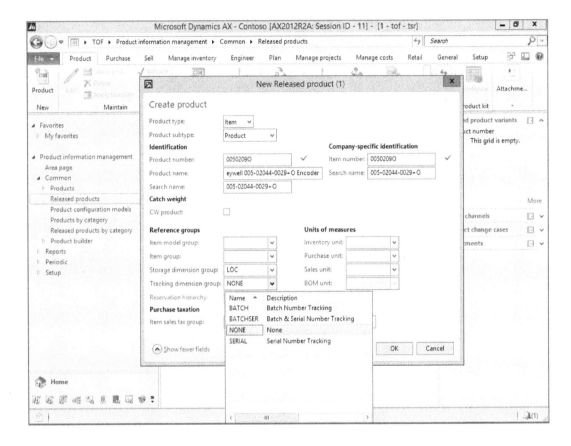

Then click on the **Tracking Dimension Group** dropdown and select the tracking dimension of **NONE** since we will not be using batch or serial number tracking on this item.

Creating A Product

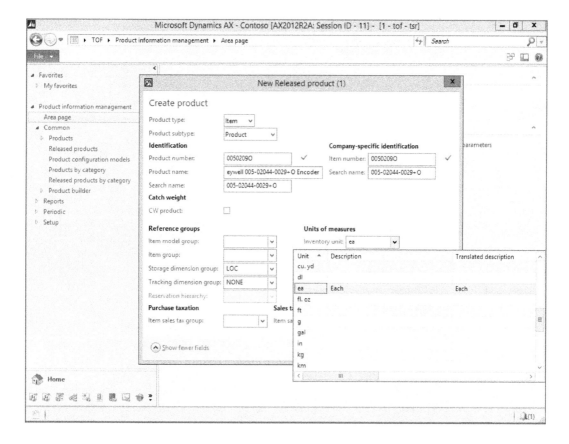

Now click on the **Inventory Unit** dropdown box and select the **ea Unit Of Measure** that we just configured.

Creating A Product

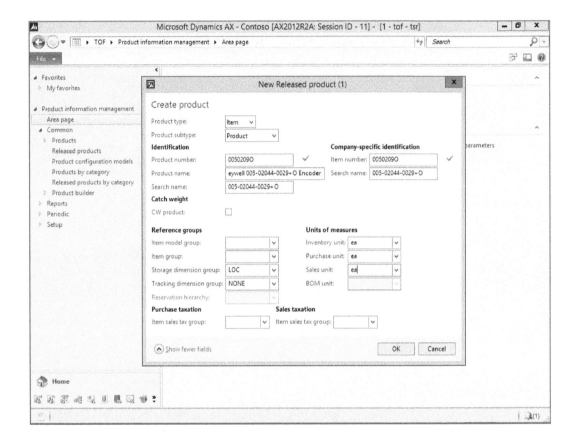

Then set the **Purchase Unit** and the **Sales Unit** to **ea** as well.

Now that you have done that, just click on the **OK** button to create the product and you are done.

Manually Updating Product Details

After you have created your **Product** you can now update all of the other product information through the maintenance forms.

Manually Updating Product Details

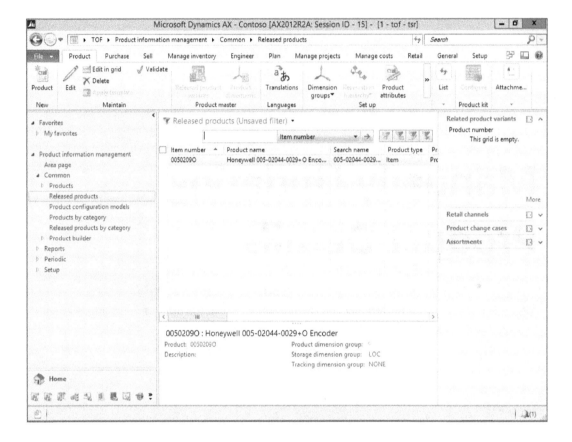

To do this return to the **Released Products** list page, and either double click on the item that you want to edit, or select the product and click on the **Edit** button within the **Maintain** group of the **Product** ribbon bar.

Manually Updating Product Details

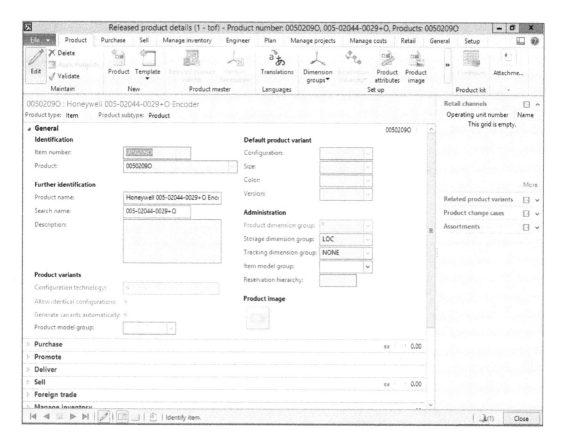

This will open up the product details form and you will see that there is a lot more information available to you.

Manually Updating Product Details

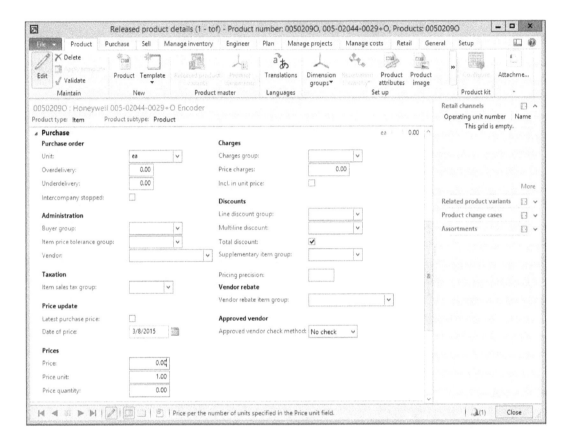

One thing that you may want to do is to set the default **Purchase Price** on the product. To do this, expand out the **Purchase** tab group so that you can see all of the purchasing fields.

Manually Updating Product Details

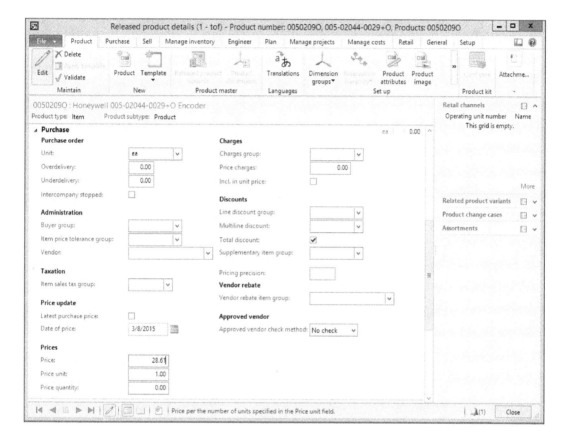

Now change the **Price** field within the Prices field group to **26.61**.

da×c

Manually Updating Product Details

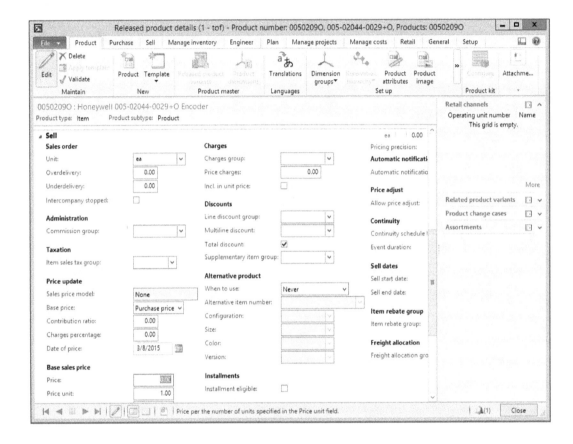

Then scroll down and open up the **Sell** tab group.

Manually Updating Product Details

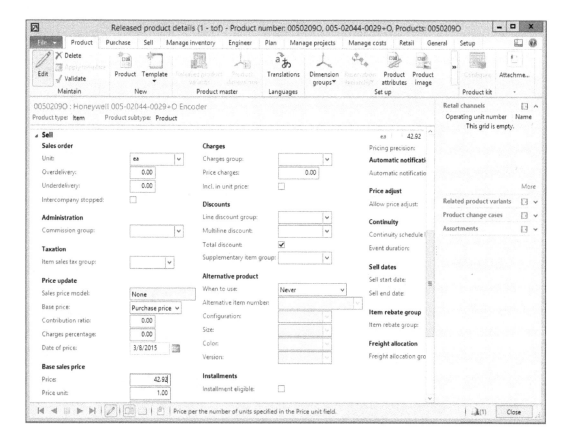

Then change the **Price** field within the **Base Sales Prices** field group to **42.92**.

You can keep on tweaking the data within your product as much as you like.

Adding A Product Image

Something else that you may want to do with your product is add a product image to the record to give users a more visual view of the product.

Adding A Product Image

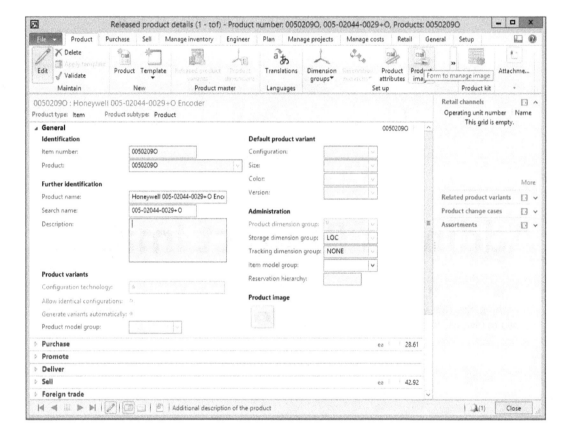

To do this, click on the **Product Image** button within the **Setup** group of the **Product** ribbon bar.

Adding A Product Image

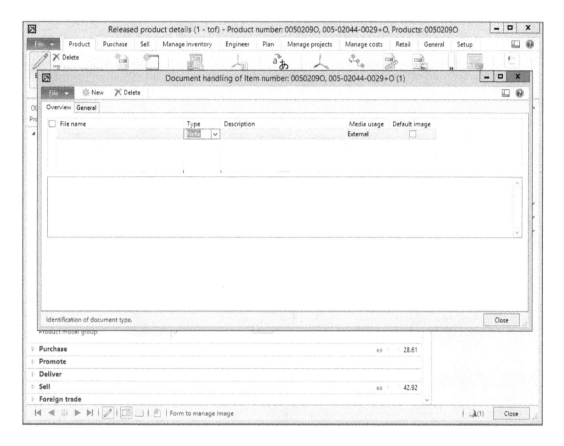

When the **Document Handling** dialog box is displayed, click on the **New** button in the menu bar to create a new record.

Adding A Product Image

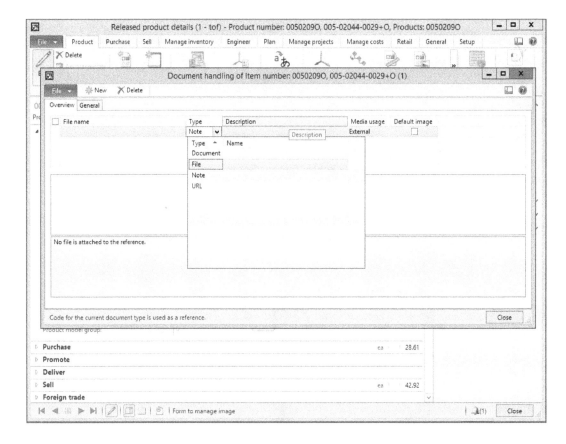

Then click on the dropdown list for the **Type** field and select the **File** record.

Adding A Product Image

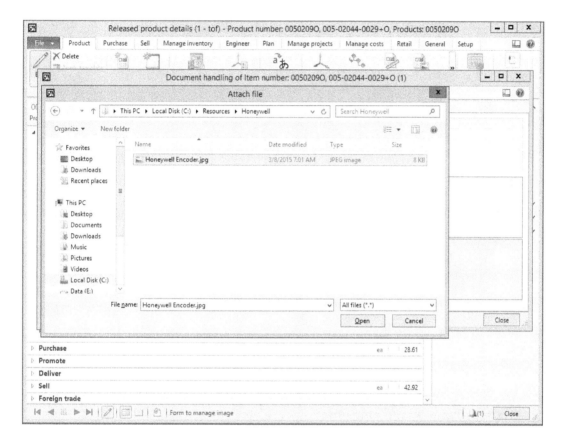

This will open up a file explorer for you and you can browse to the location that you have your product image stored in and then click on the **Open** button.

daxc

Adding A Product Image

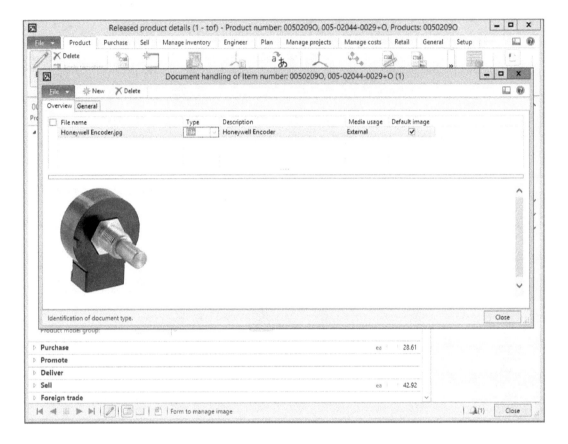

When you return back to the **Document Handling** form you will be able to see the image in the bottom of the window. If it is not already checked, check the **Default Image** flag and then click on the **Close** button to exit from the form

Adding A Product Image

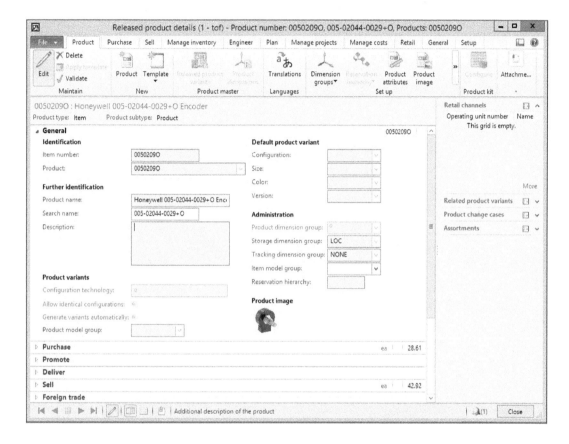

When you return back to the **Released Product Details** form you will also see that the product image is shown in the General tab group.

How cool is that?

Importing Products Using The Data Import Export Framework

Adding products by hand is pretty easy, but if you have a lot of products that you want to load into Dynamics AX, then you may want to use the **Data Import Export Framework** to load them in from a CSV file, or an Excel spreadsheet.

Importing Products Using The Data Import Export Framework

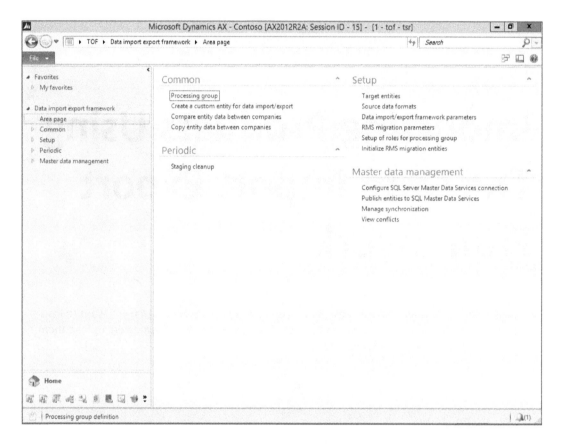

To do this, click on the **Processing Group** menu item within the **Common** group of the **Data Import Export Framework** area page.

Importing Products Using The Data Import Export Framework

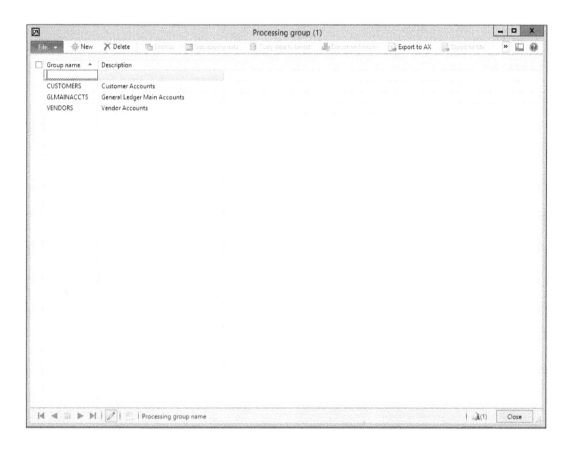

When the **Processing Group** list form is displayed, click on the **New** button within the menu bar to create a new record.

Importing Products Using The Data Import Export Framework

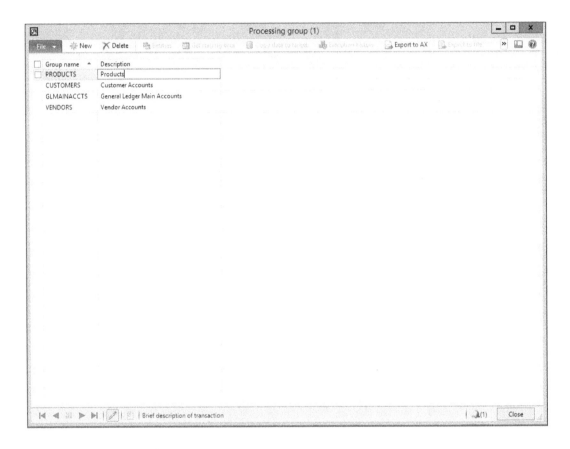

Then set the **Group Name** to **Products** and the **Description** to **Products.**

Importing Products Using The Data Import Export Framework

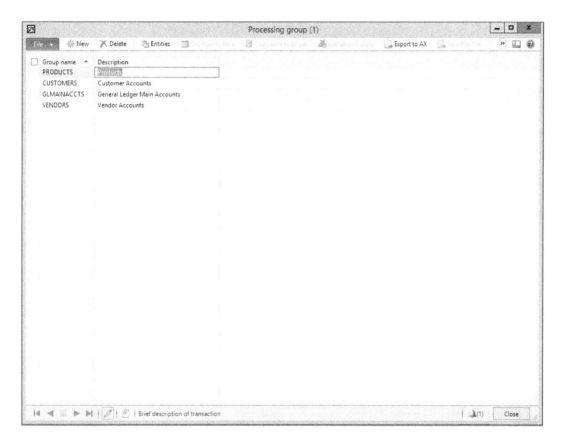

Then press **CTRL+S** to save the record. That will enable the **Entities** button within the menu bar and you can then click on it.

Importing Products Using The Data Import Export Framework

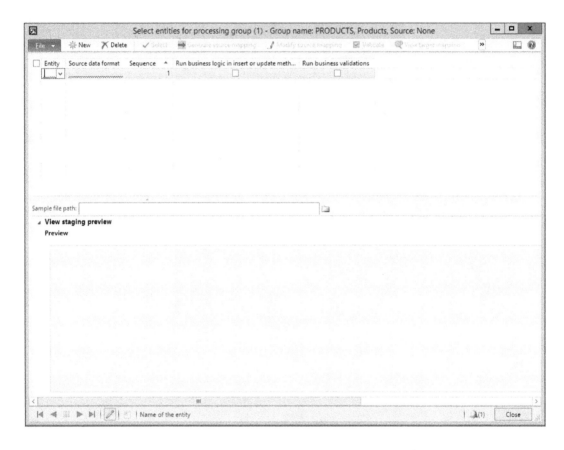

This will open up the **Select Entities For Processing Group** maintenance form.

Importing Products Using The Data Import Export Framework

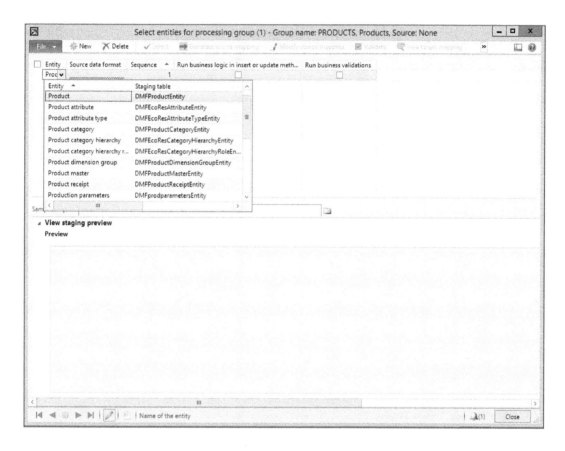

Click on the dropdown list for the **Entity** field and select the **Product** record.

Importing Products Using The Data Import Export Framework

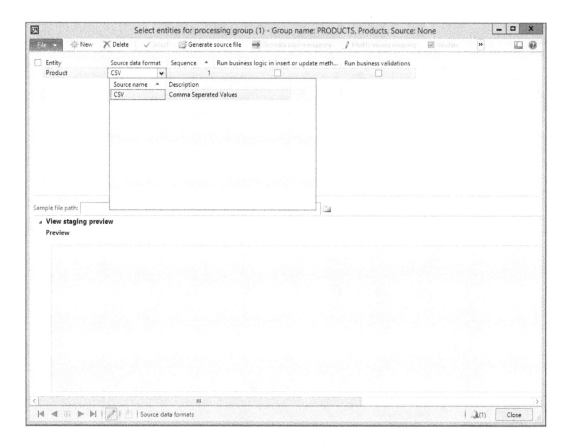

Then select the **CSV** option from the **Source Data Format** dropdown list.

Importing Products Using The Data Import Export Framework

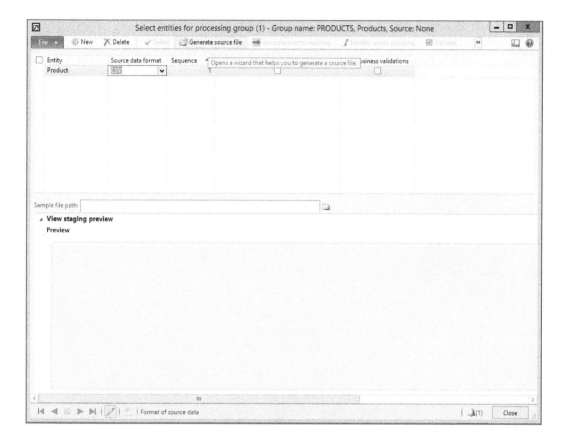

Then click on the **Generate Source File** button within the menu bar.

Importing Products Using The Data Import Export Framework

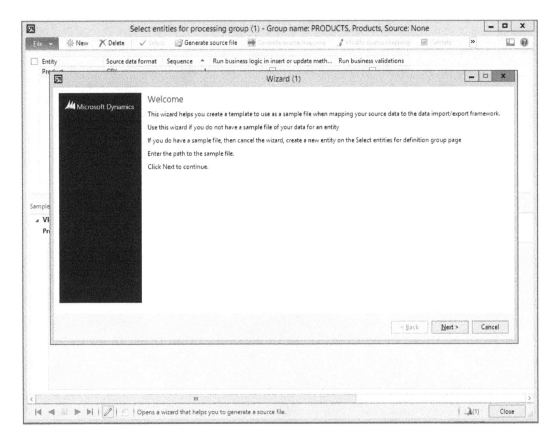

This will open up the **Source File Generation Wizard** form. Click on the **Next** button to skip past the introduction page.

Importing Products Using The Data Import Export Framework

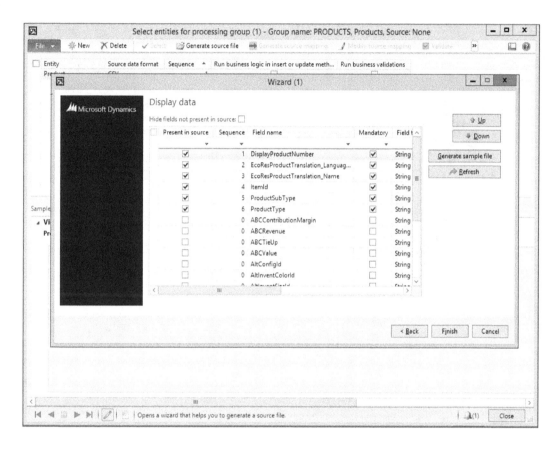

When the **Display Data** page is displayed you will see that it has already selected a set of default fields that you will want to load for the product.

We just need to add a few more fields. There is a trick that you may want to do though rather than searching through all of the fields manually. If you press **CTRL+G** then a filter bar will be displayed at the top of the grid.

Importing Products Using The Data Import Export Framework

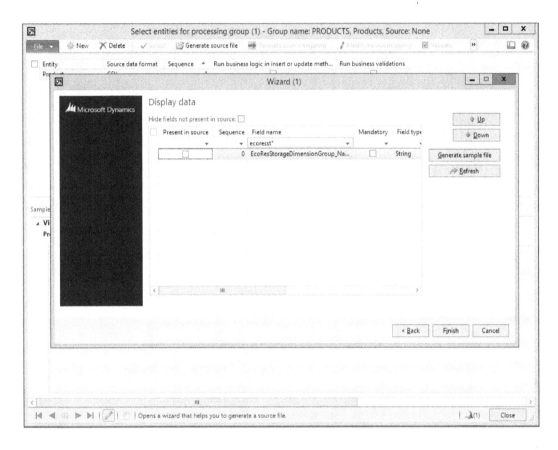

Now just type in **ecoresst*** to find the **EcoResStorageDimensionGroupName** field and check the **Present In Source** flag.

Importing Products Using The Data Import Export Framework

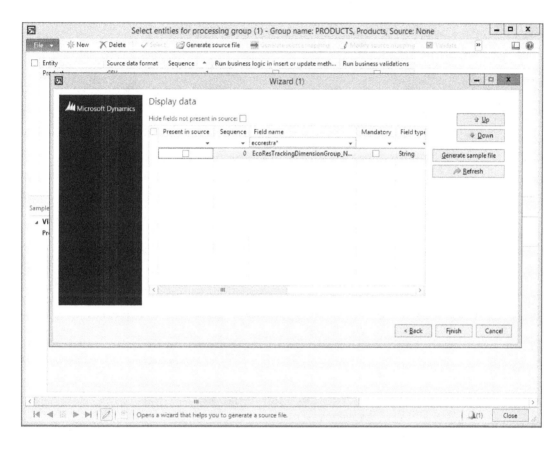

Then type in **ecorestr*** to find the **EcoResTrackingDimensionGroupName** field and check the **Present In Source** flag.

Importing Products Using The Data Import Export Framework

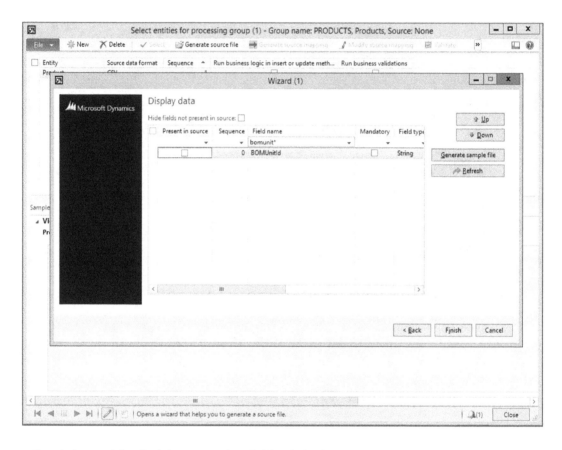

Type in **bomunit*** to find the **BOMUnitID** field and check the **Present In Source** flag.

Importing Products Using The Data Import Export Framework

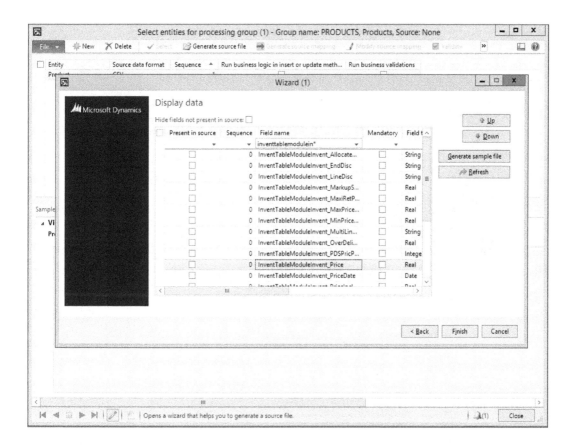

The next few are a little bit more work. Start off by typing in **inventtablemodulein*.** You will get a larger list which you will see the **InventTableModuleInvent_Price** field and you can check the **Present In Source** flag.

Importing Products Using The Data Import Export Framework

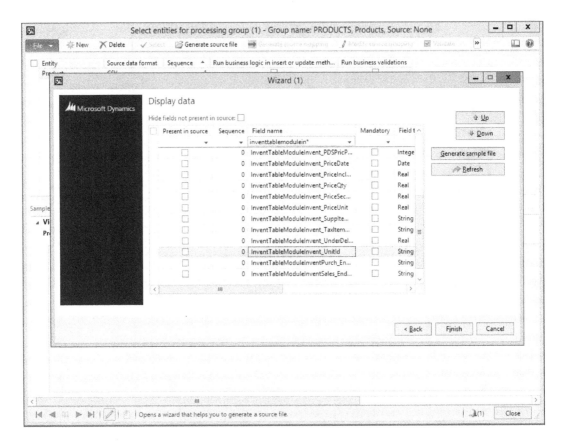

Type in **inventtablemodulein*** again, and this time select the
InventTableModuleInvent_UnitId field and you can check the **Present In Source** flag.

Importing Products Using The Data Import Export Framework

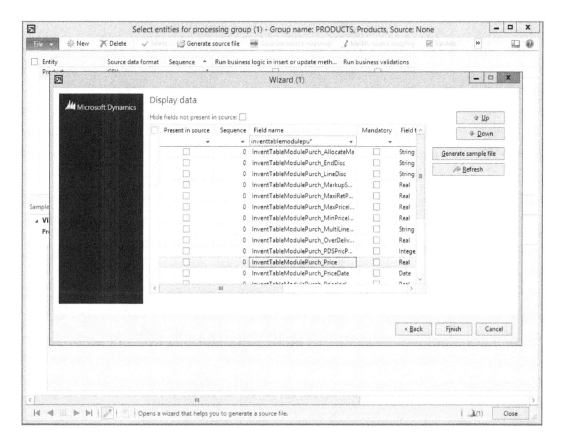

Type in **inventtablemodulepu***, and this time select the **InventTableModulePurch_Price** field and you can check the **Present In Source** flag.

Importing Products Using The Data Import Export Framework

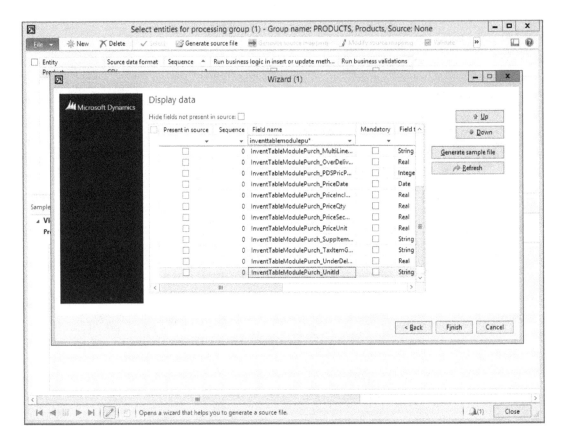

Type in **inventtablemodulepu*** again, and this time select the **InventTableModulePurch_UnitId** field and you can check the **Present In Source** flag.

da*c

Importing Products Using The Data Import Export Framework

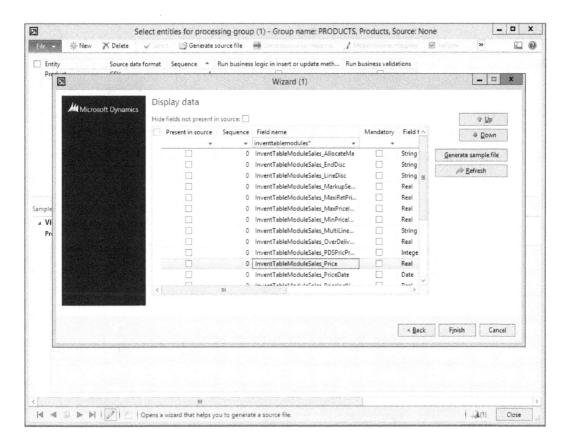

Type in **inventtablemodulesa***, and this time select the **InventTableModuleSales_Price** field and you can check the **Present In Source** flag.

Importing Products Using The Data Import Export Framework

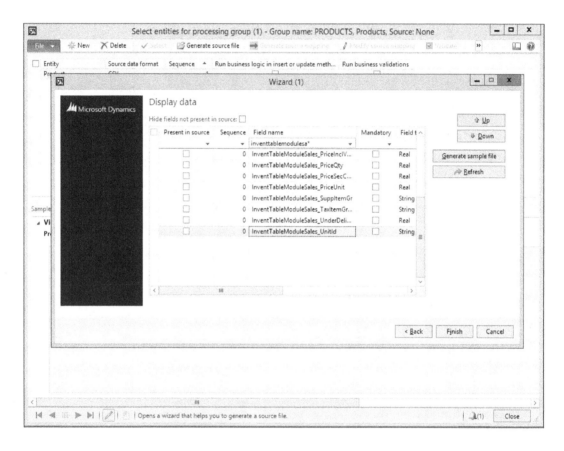

And type in **inventtablemodulepu* again**, and this time select the
InventTableModulePurch_UnitId field and you can check the **Present In Source** flag.

Importing Products Using The Data Import Export Framework

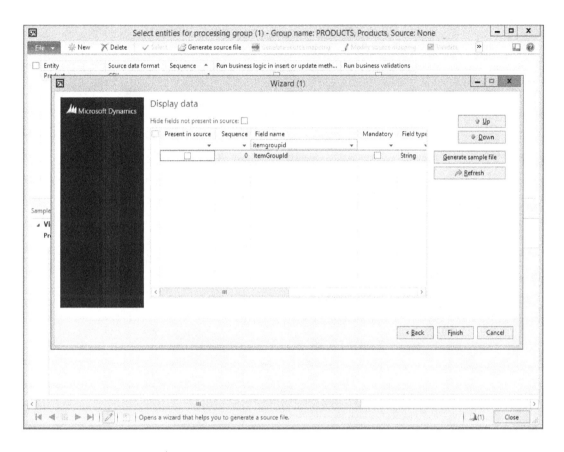

Type in **itemgroupid*** and check the **Present In Source** flag for the **ItemGroupId** field.

Importing Products Using The Data Import Export Framework

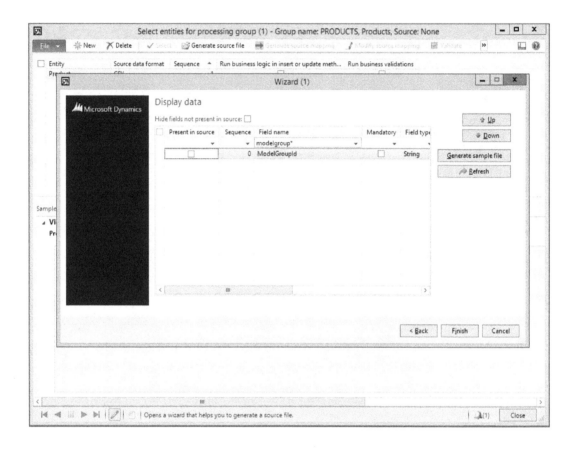

Type in **modelgroup*** and check the **Present In Source** flag for the **ModelGroupId** field.

Importing Products Using The Data Import Export Framework

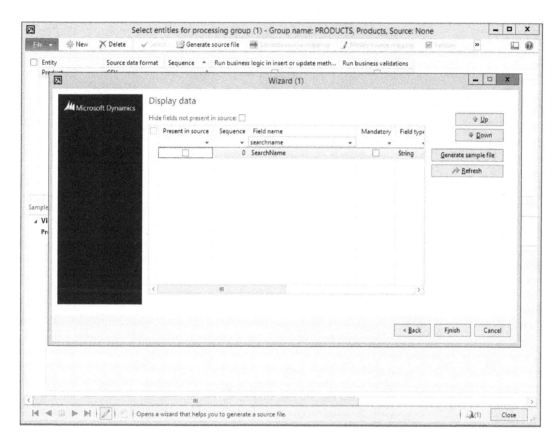

Type in **searchname*** and check the **Present In Source** flag for the **SearchName** field.

Importing Products Using The Data Import Export Framework

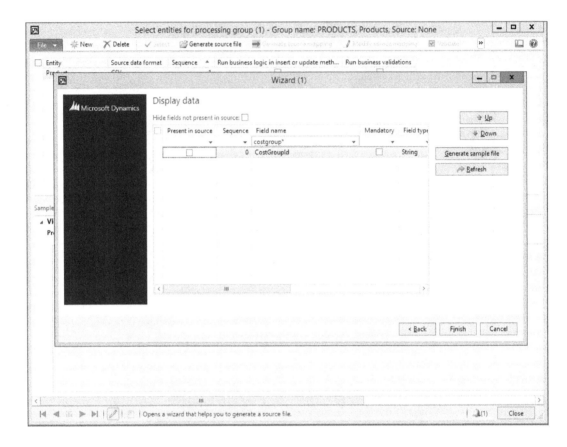

Type in **costgroup*** and check the **Present In Source** flag for the **CostGroupId** field.

Importing Products Using The Data Import Export Framework

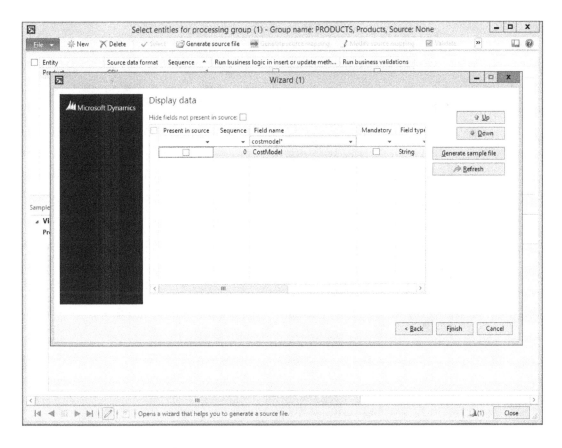

Type in **costmodel*** and check the **Present In Source** flag for the **CostModel** field.

Importing Products Using The Data Import Export Framework

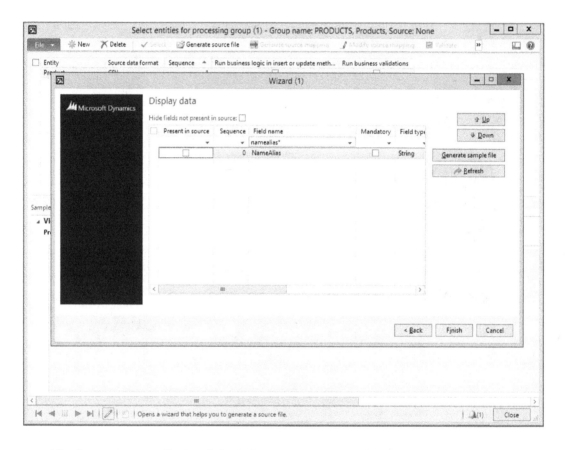

And finally type in **namealias*** and check the **Present In Source** flag for the **NameAlias** field.

Importing Products Using The Data Import Export Framework

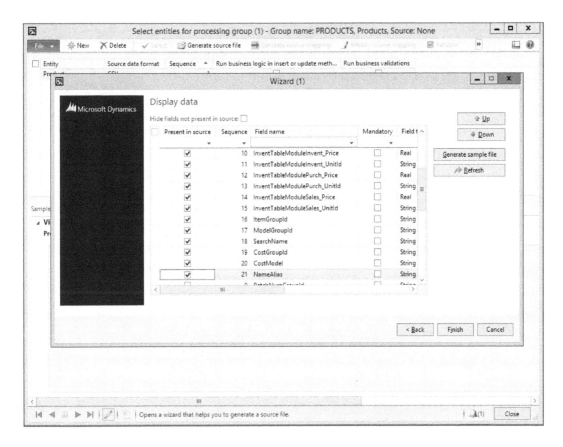

After you have selected all of the fields that you need, click on the **Generate Sample File** button to the right of the form.

Importing Products Using The Data Import Export Framework

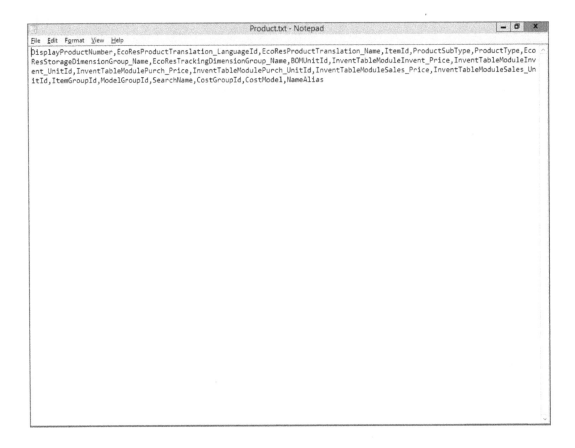

This will open up **Notepad** with the CSV template for the import.

Importing Products Using The Data Import Export Framework

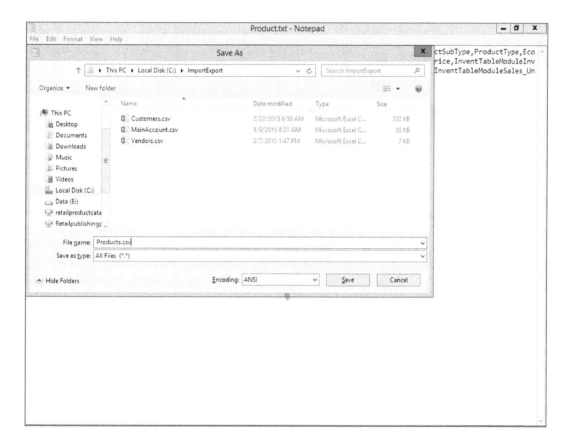

Just save the file away to the default Import/Export folder as a **.csv** extension.

Note: You will need to change the **Save As Type** to **All Files (*.*)** otherwise you will save the file as a text file.

Importing Products Using The Data Import Export Framework

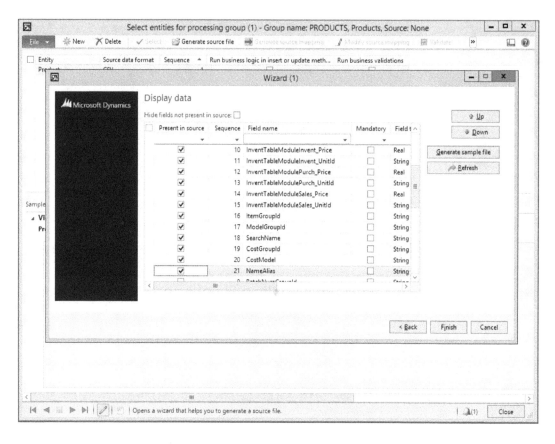

When you return back to the **Display Data** form, just click on the **Finish** button to complete the wizard.

Importing Products Using The Data Import Export Framework

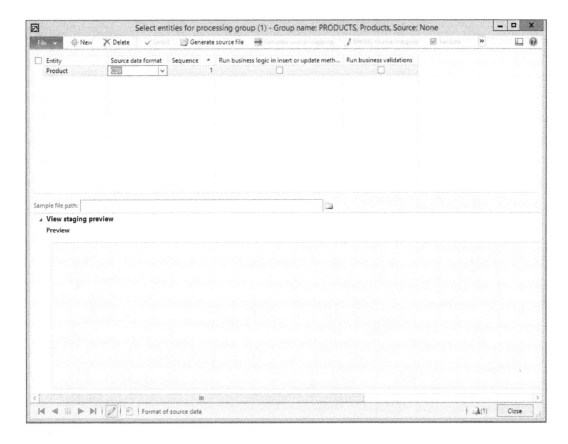

When you return back to the **Select Entities for Processing Group** form, click on the **Folder** icon to the right of the **Sample File Path** field.

Importing Products Using The Data Import Export Framework

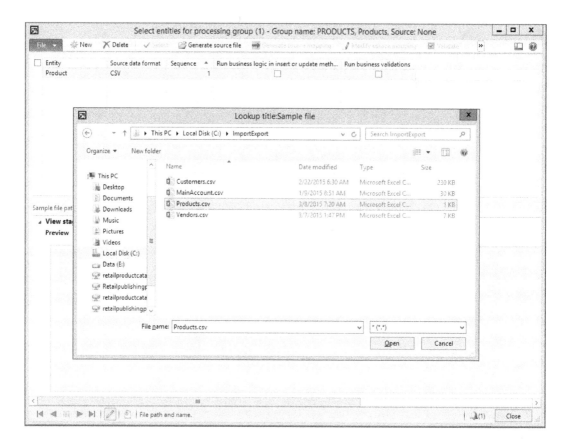

This will open up a file explorer and you will be able to navigate to your new **Products.csv** file that you just saved away and click on the **Open** button.

Importing Products Using The Data Import Export Framework

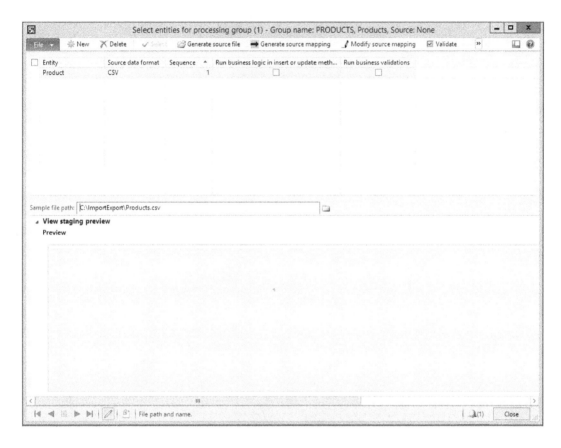

When you return back to the **Select Entities for Processing Group** form, click on the **Generate Source Mapping** button in the menu bar.

Importing Products Using The Data Import Export Framework

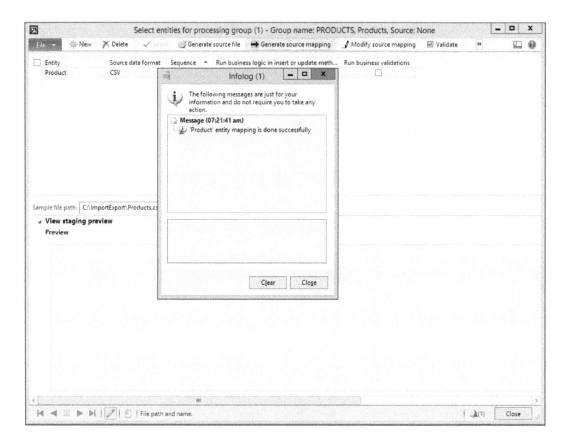

An InfoLog will pop up saying that the data maps have been created and you can click on the **Close** button.

Importing Products Using The Data Import Export Framework

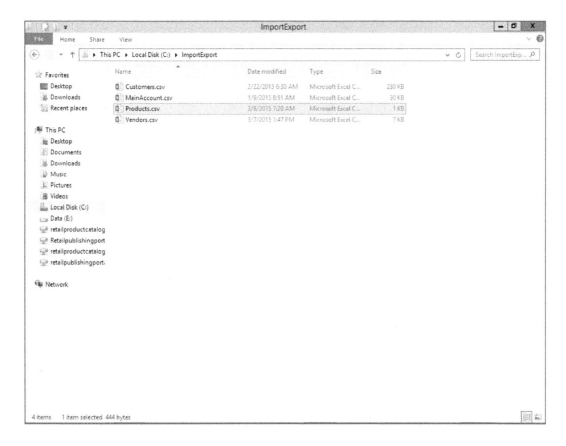

Now open up a **File Explorer** and find the **Products.csv** file that you just created as a template and open it.

Importing Products Using The Data Import Export Framework

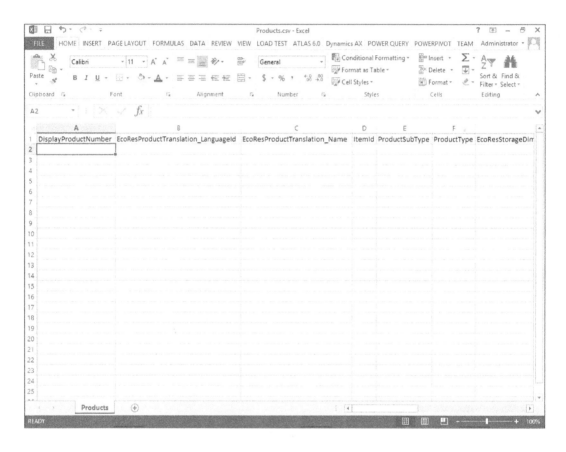

This will open the import file for you all you need to do is start filling in all of the columns.

Importing Products Using The Data Import Export Framework

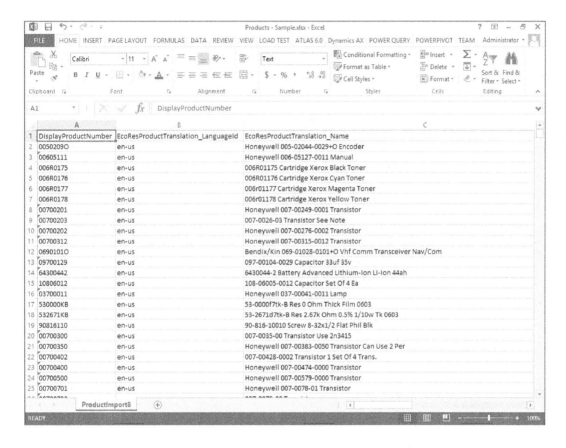

To save time, we have created a small product sample list for you all that you can download from the **Dynamics AX Companions** (www.dynamicsaxcompanions.com) website for you that you can download.

Importing Products Using The Data Import Export Framework

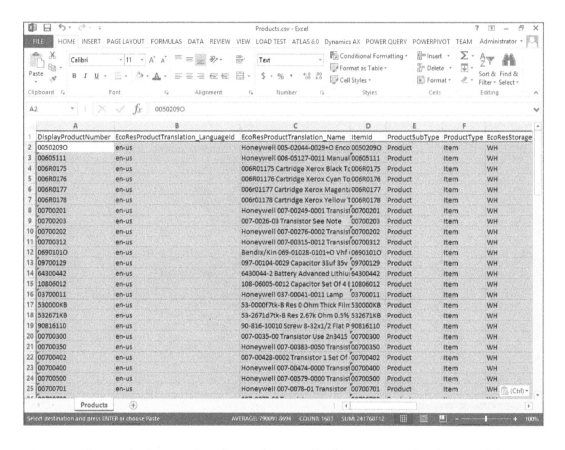

Just copy the sample data over into the **Products.csv** file that you opened and save and close the file.

Importing Products Using The Data Import Export Framework

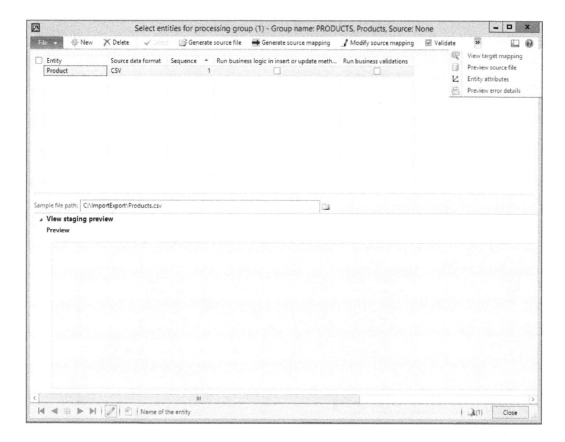

Now return to the **Select Criteria For Processing Groups** maintenance form and click on the **Preview Source File** button in the menu bar.

Tip: If you have smaller real-estate on your screen then you may need to click on the **>>** button to see all of the hidden menu items.

Importing Products Using The Data Import Export Framework

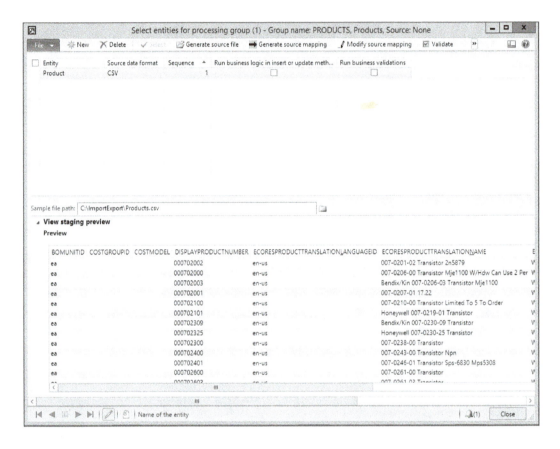

If all of your fields are in the correct order then you will see all of the products in the **Preview** table at the bottom of the form and you can click on the **Close** button to exit from the form.

Importing Products Using The Data Import Export Framework

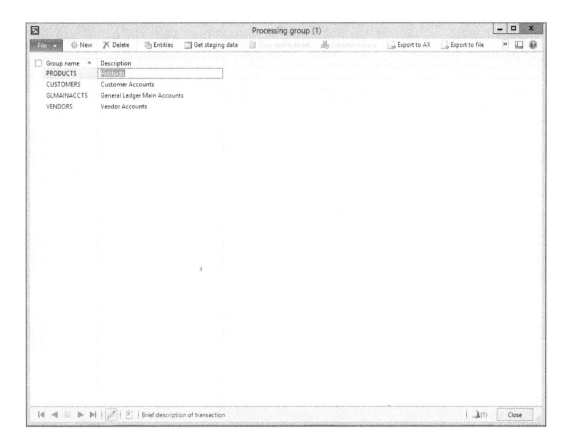

When you return to the **Processing Groups** maintenance form, click on the **Get Staging Data** button in the menu bar.

Importing Products Using The Data Import Export Framework

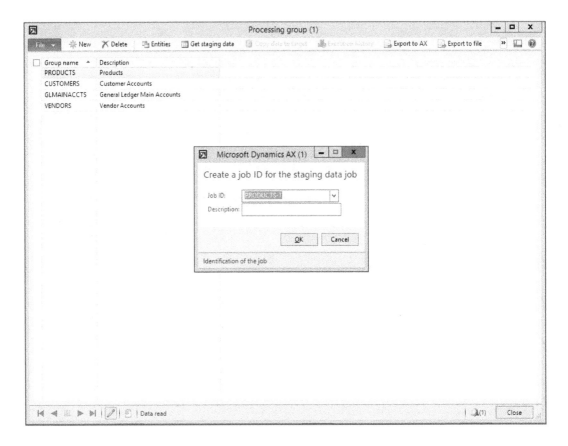

When the **Create a Job** dialog box is displayed, click on the **OK** button.

Importing Products Using The Data Import Export Framework

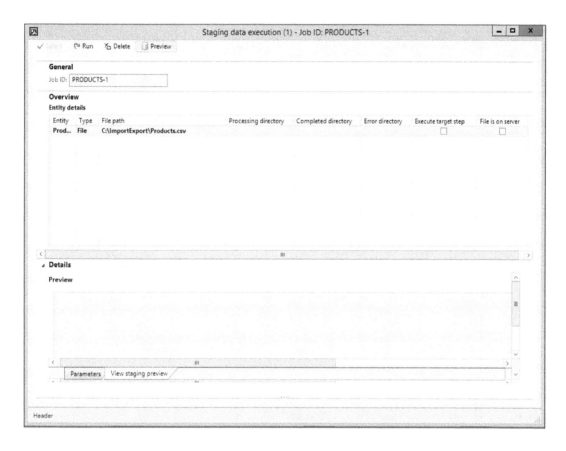

This will open up the **Staging Data Execution** maintenance form. Just to make sure everything is still fine, click on the **Preview** button in the menu bar.

Importing Products Using The Data Import Export Framework

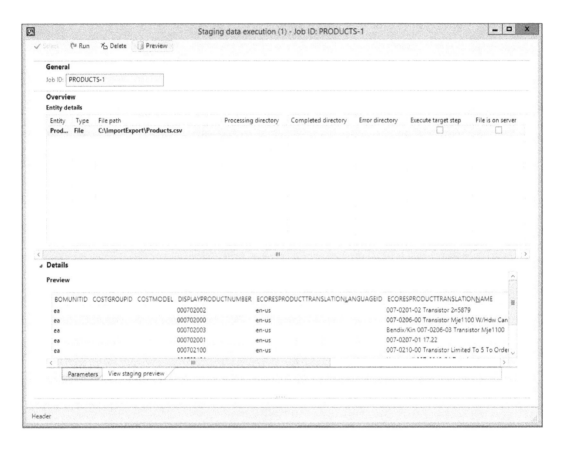

Within the **Details** tab group, on the **View Staging Preview** footer tab you should get a sample set of data.

This looks good so now lets click on the **Run** button in the menu bar to start the import of the data into the staging area.

Importing Products Using The Data Import Export Framework

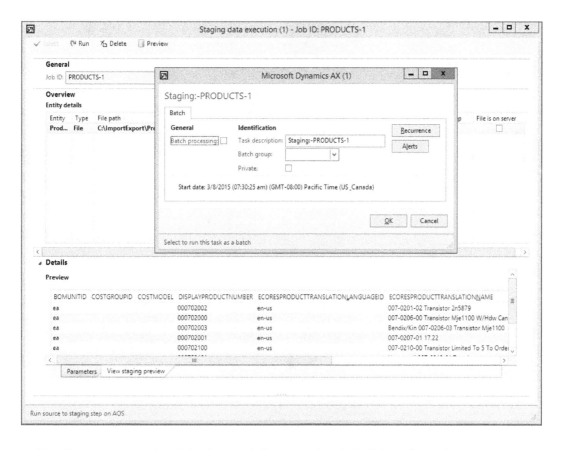

This will open up a **Staging** dialog box, and all you need to do is click on the **OK** button.

Importing Products Using The Data Import Export Framework

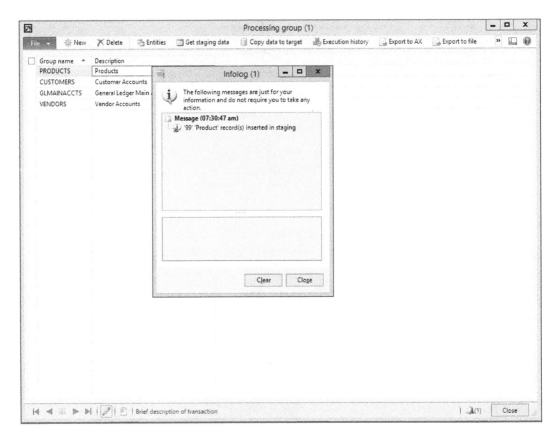

You will then get an **InfoLog** that shows you how many products were put into staging ans you can click the **Close** button to exit from it.

Importing Products Using The Data Import Export Framework

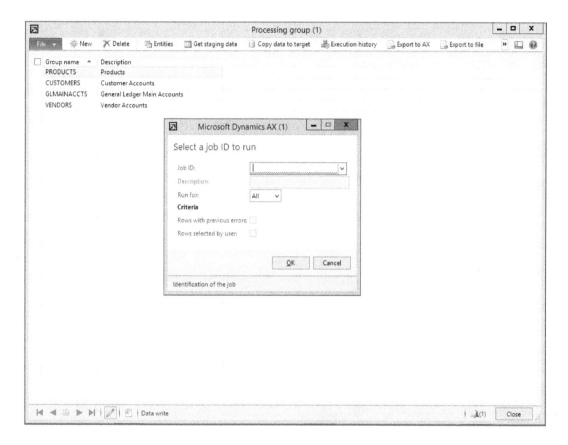

Now the **Copy Data To Target** button will be enabled within the menu bar and you will be able to click it and open up the **Select A Job** dialog box.

Importing Products Using The Data Import Export Framework

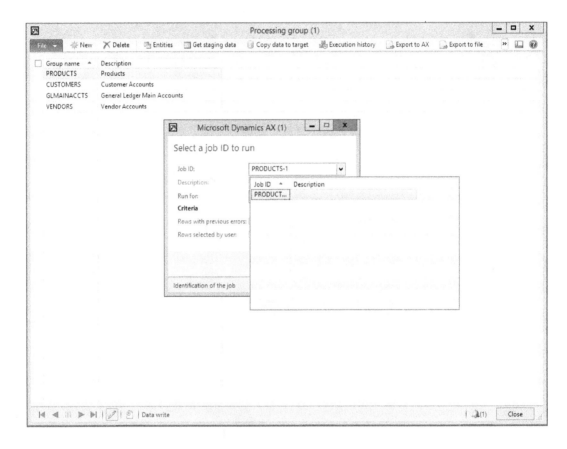

Select the **Job ID** that you just created from the dropdown list.

Importing Products Using The Data Import Export Framework

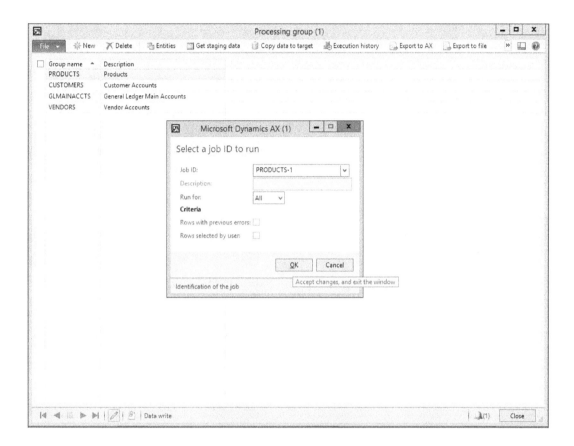

And then click on the **OK** button.

Importing Products Using The Data Import Export Framework

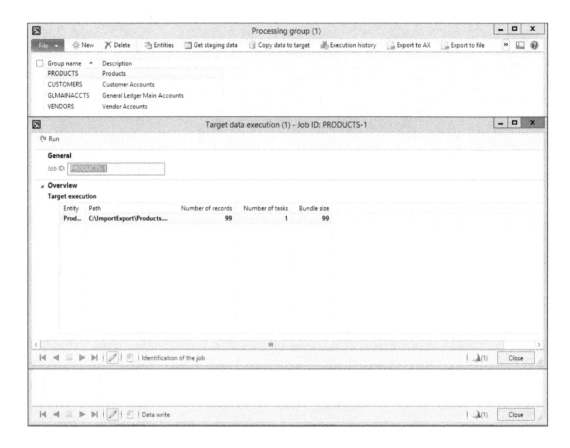

When the **Target Data Execution** form is displayed, click on the **Run** button within the menu bar to start moving the data over into the Products table.

Importing Products Using The Data Import Export Framework

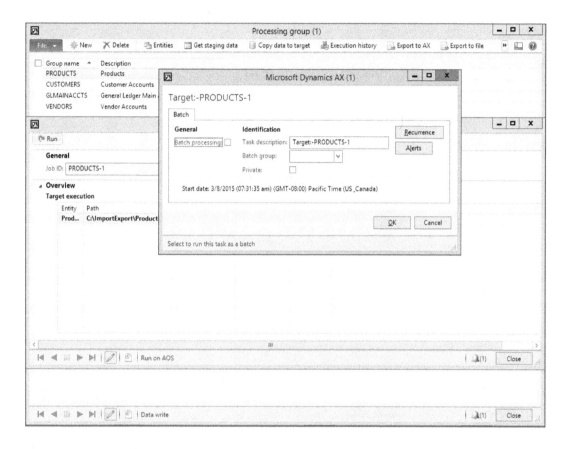

When the **Target** dislog box is displayed, just click on the **OK** button.

Importing Products Using The Data Import Export Framework

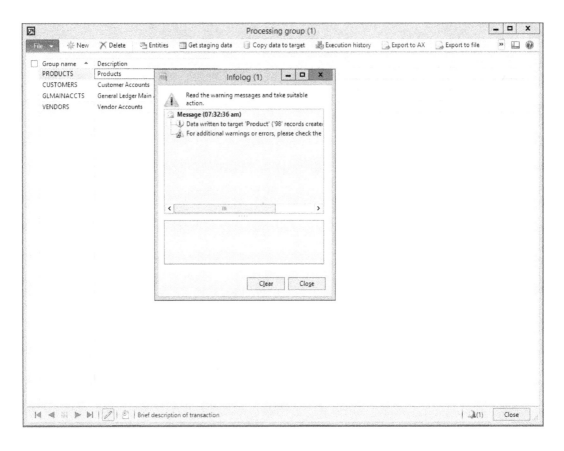

This will give you an **InfoLog** box showing you the status of the data load. When you are done, just click on the **Close** button to return to the **Processing Groups** and then click the **Close** button on that form to exit out of it as well.

Importing Products Using The Data Import Export Framework

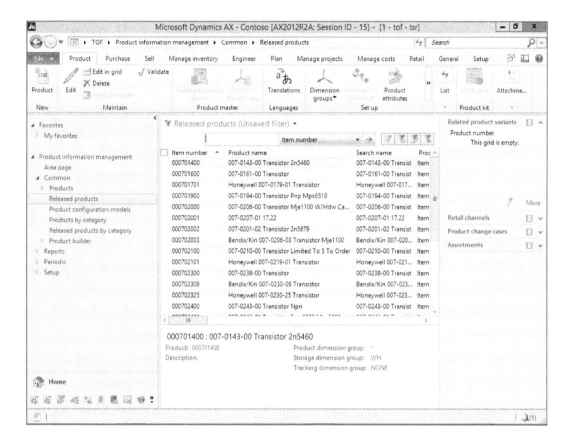

When you return to the **Released Products** list page you will see that there is a lot more data there for you.

Importing Products Using The Data Import Export Framework

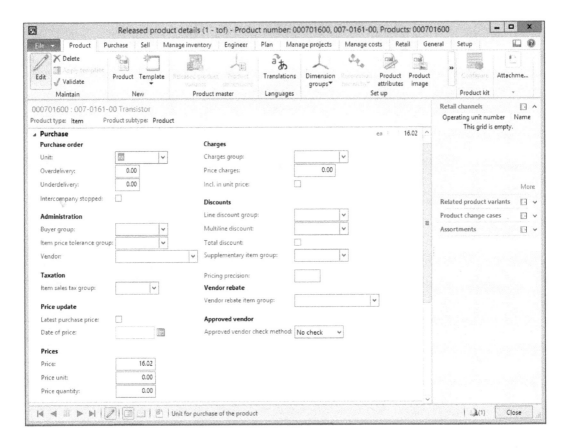

If you open up any of the products as well, you will see that some of the key information is already loaded for you – like the **Purchase** and **Sales** prices.

Now that was easy!

Creating A Service Item

The products that we have been creating up until now have been physical items, but that doesn't mean that is the only type that you can use. You can also create **Service** products as well which bypass all of the inventory tracking and physical requirements of the tangible products.

Creating A Service Item

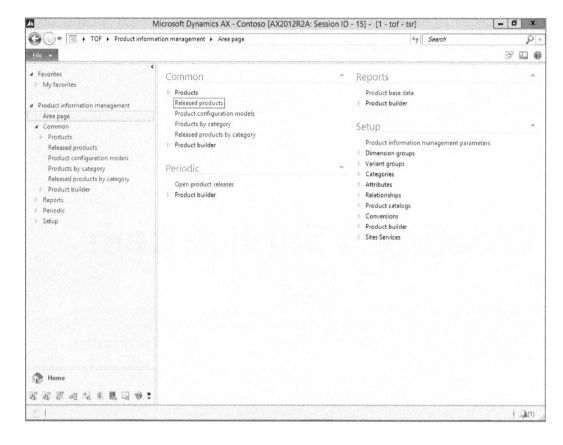

You create a **Service** product almost exactly the same way as you do for a physical product. Start off by clicking on the **Released Products** menu item within the **Common** group of the **Product Information Management** area page.

Creating A Service Item

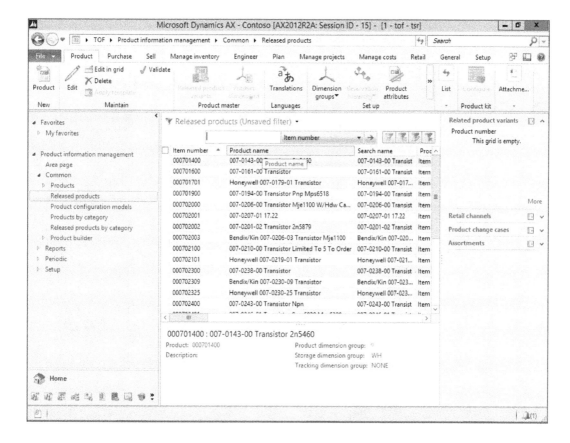

When the **Released Products** list page is displayed, click on the **Product** button within the **New** group of the **Products** ribbon bar.

Creating A Service Item

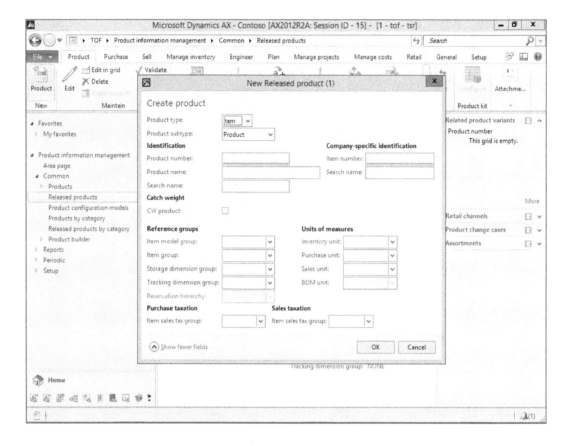

This will open up the **New Released Product** dialog box that you used in the previous example.

Creating A Service Item

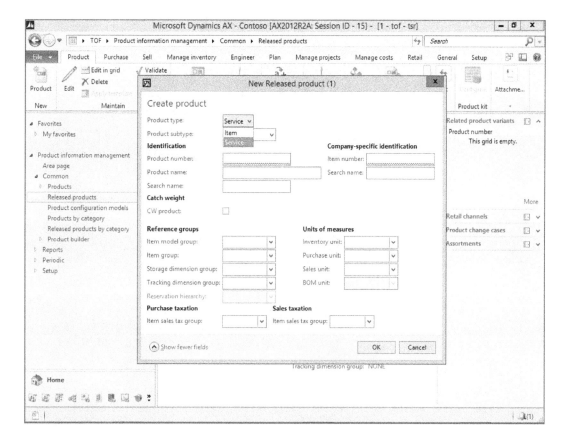

To create a **Service** product, just click on the **Product Type** dropdown list and select the **Service** option.

Creating A Service Item

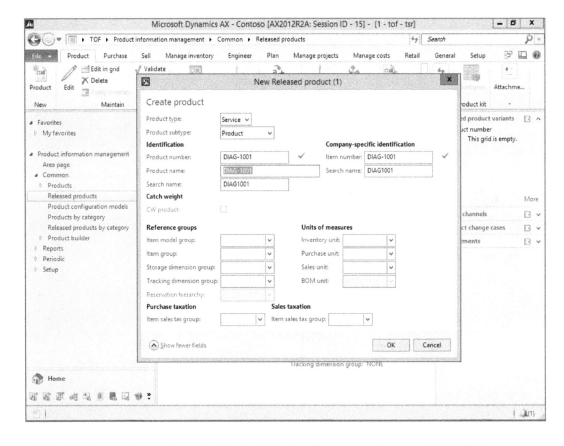

This will allow you to then type in a **Product Number** for your service – use **DIAG-1001**.

Creating A Service Item

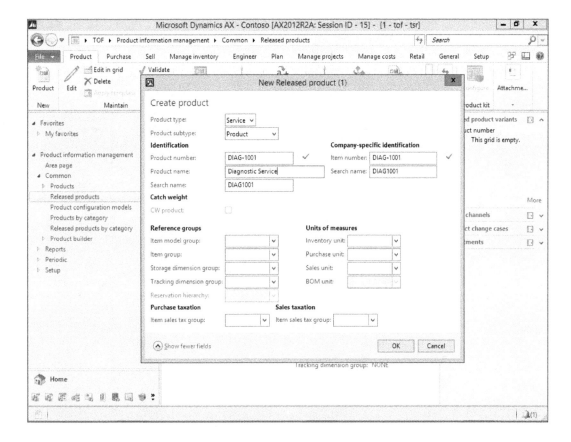

And then change the **Product Name** to **Diagnostic Service**.

Creating A Service Item

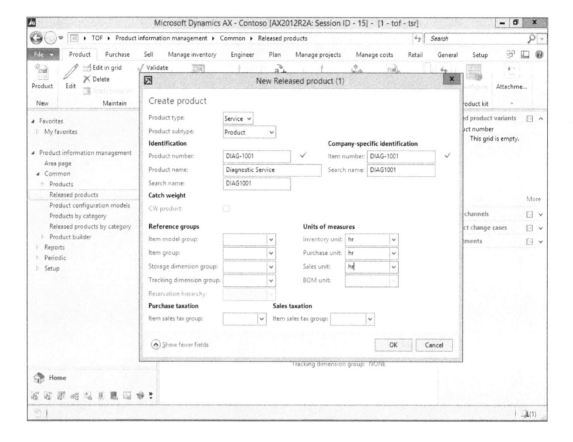

Then update the **Units Of Measure** for **Inventory**, **Purchase**, and **Sales** to **hr**.

Note: I don't think that you really need to specify the **Inventory Unit** but it looks tidier.

When you have done that, click on the **OK** button to complete the setup.

Creating A Service Item

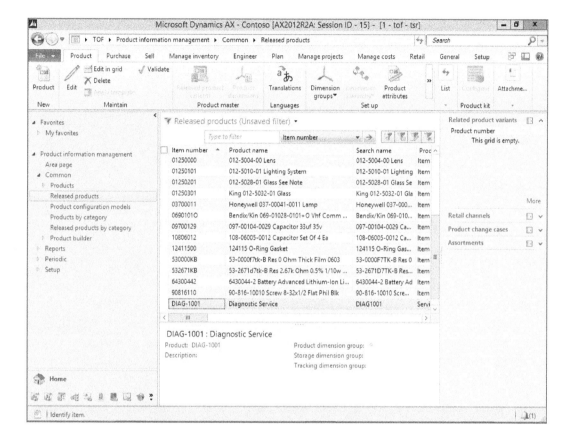

When you return back to the **Released Products** list page you will see that you now have a Service item.

Creating A Service Item

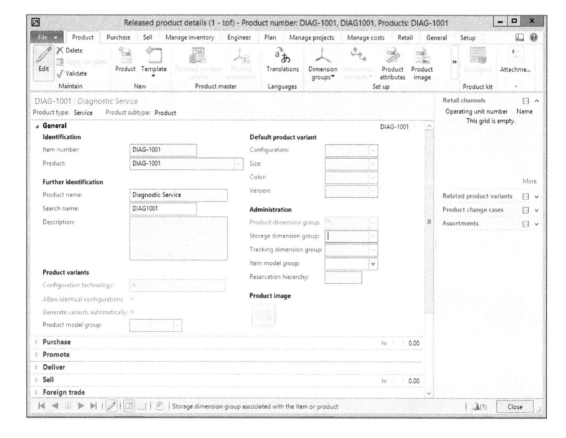

If you open up the record then you can update it just the same way as you do for a physical product.

How easy is that?

Creating Product Templates

If you have products that are almost the same in their configurations except for some small tweaks here and there, then you can save a little bit of time by creating a master template for the products from one that is already set up and then use it when you create new products.

Creating Product Templates

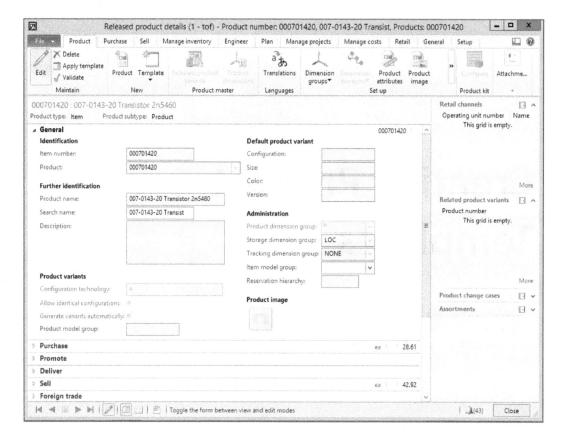

To do this, start off my opening up the Released Product record that is going to be used as the master for the template.

Creating Product Templates

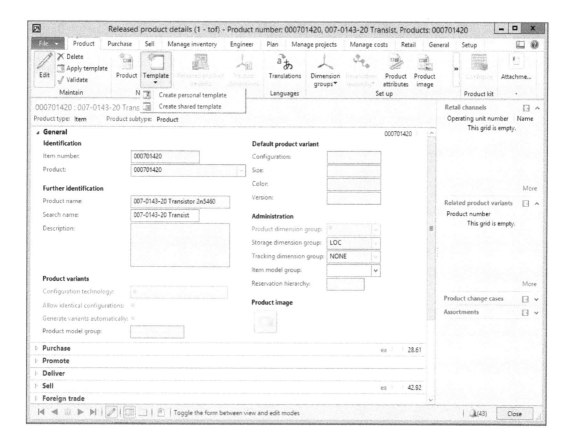

Then click on the **Template** button within the **New** group of the **Product** ribbon bar, and select the **Create Personal Template**. If you want to share the template with everyone else then you can select the **Create Shared Template** I guess.

Creating Product Templates

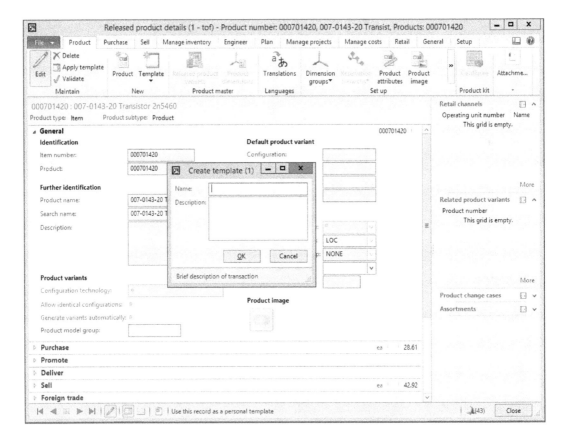

This will open up a **Create Template** dialog box.

Creating Product Templates

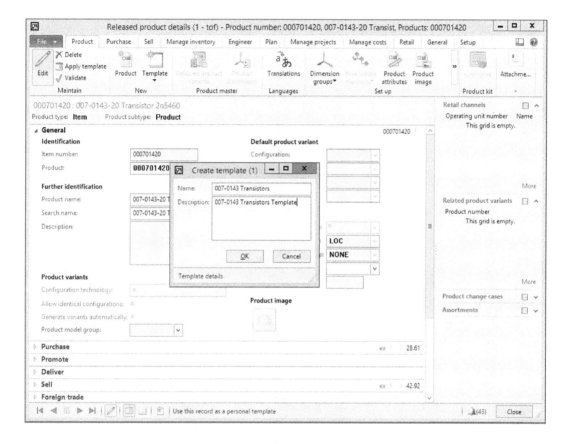

Just give your template a **Name** and a **Description** and press the **OK** button.

And you are done.

Creating New Products Using Product Templates

You can use the templates that you create a couple of different ways. The first that we will look at is the ability to select the template as you are creating the product records, and have all of the template details default in for you.

Creating New Products Using Product Templates

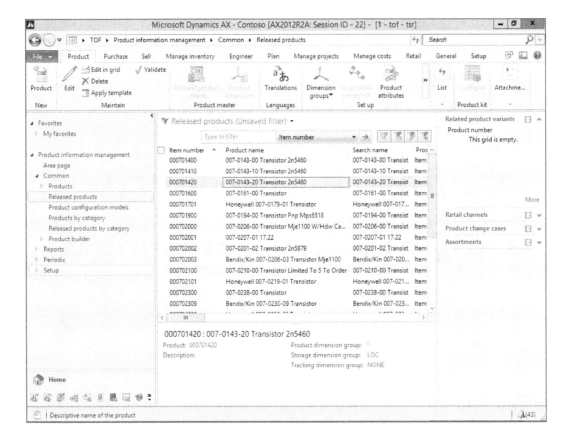

To do this, open up the **Released Products** list page and click on the **Product** button in the **New** group of the **Product** ribbon bar to create a new product.

Creating New Products Using Product Templates

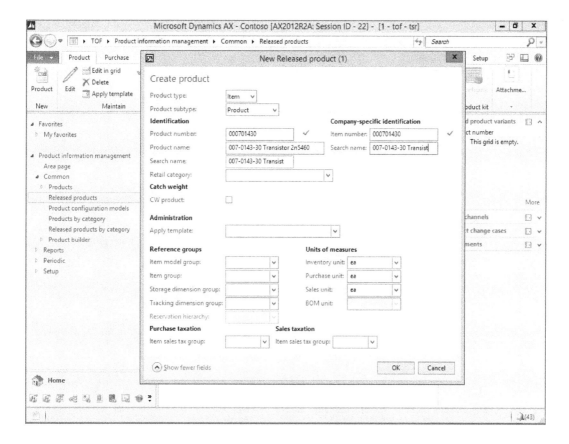

Then the **New Released Product** dialog box is displayed, type in the **Product Number**, the **Product Name**, and set the **Search Names**.

Creating New Products Using Product Templates

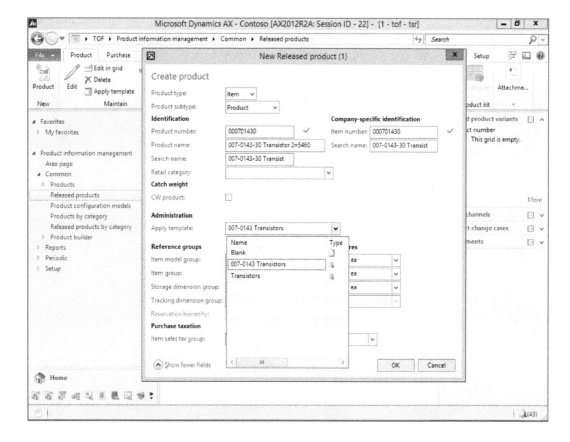

You will notice that something is a little different now that you have the templates created, there is a new field group called **Administration**.

If you click on the **Apply Template** fields dropdown list then you will see that your template is listed there and you can select it.

Creating New Products Using Product Templates

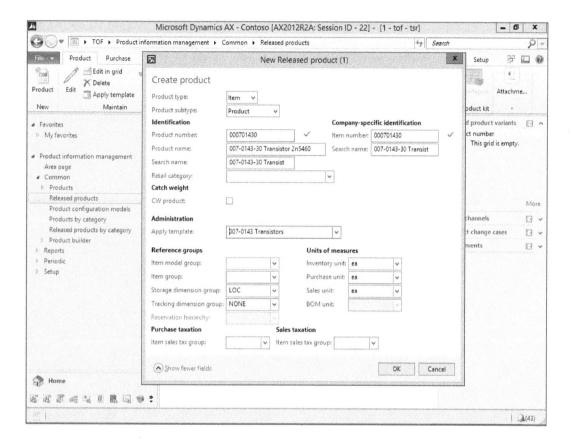

This will default in all of the codes that you had configured on the master record for you into this new record, and if everything looks good then you can just click on the **OK** button to create the new record.

Creating New Products Using Product Templates

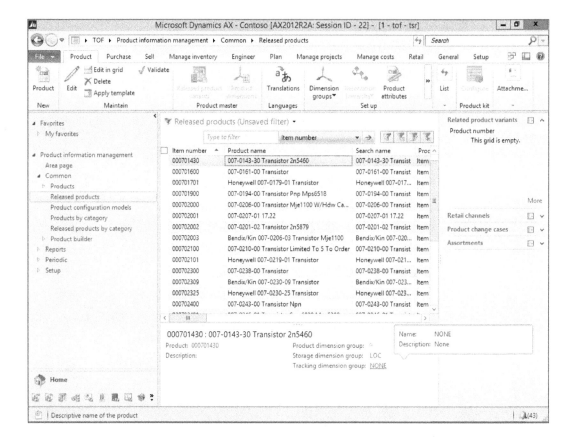

Now find the new product in the list page and open it up.

Creating New Products Using Product Templates

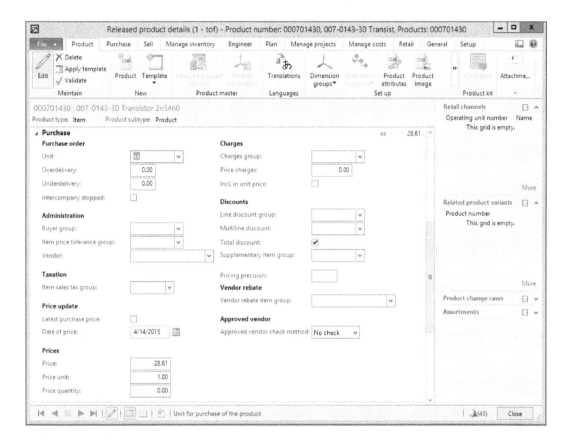

You will see that not only have the units been updated, but also the default pricing and any other fields that you may have configured.

This is a great way to quickly set up common products.

171

Applying Templates In Bulk to Multiple Records

To make this even more useful, you can also use the templates on records that already have already been created allowing you to perform mass updates on your products if you like.

Applying Templates In Bulk to Multiple Records

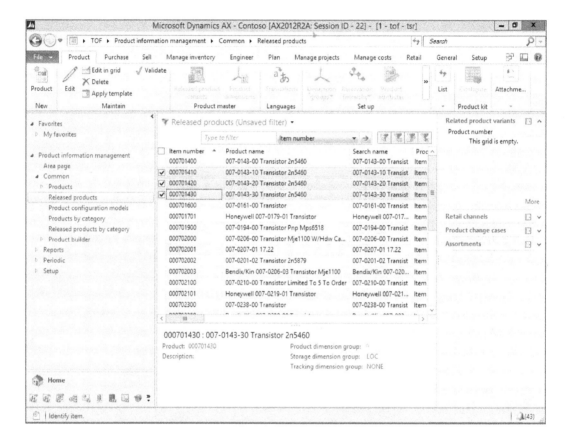

To do this, just select the products that you want to apply the template to and then click on the **Apply Template** button within the **Maintain** group of the **Product** ribbon bar.

Applying Templates In Bulk to Multiple Records

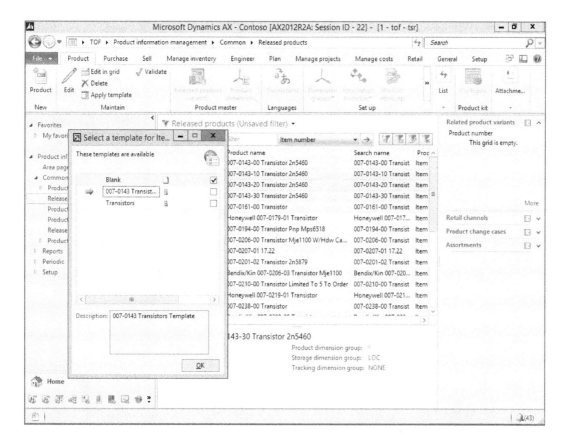

This will open up a list of all the templates that you have access top and you can select the new template and click on the **OK** button.

Applying Templates In Bulk to Multiple Records

When you return the products will be updated.

Applying Templates In Bulk to Multiple Records

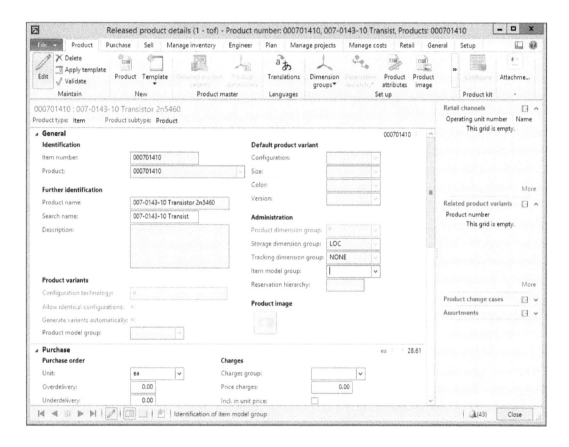

And you can drill into any of the products if you don't believe us.

Updating Product Details Using The Edit In Grid Function

If you want to perform mass updates of your products, or just want an easy way to look at all of your products and make slight tweaks to them, then you can use the **Edit In Grid** feature. This allows you to update the records as if they were a spreadsheet. You can make it even more useful by using the **Personalization** option to add additional fields that you may want to update – even if they are not on the main product table itself.

Updating Product Details Using The Edit In Grid Function

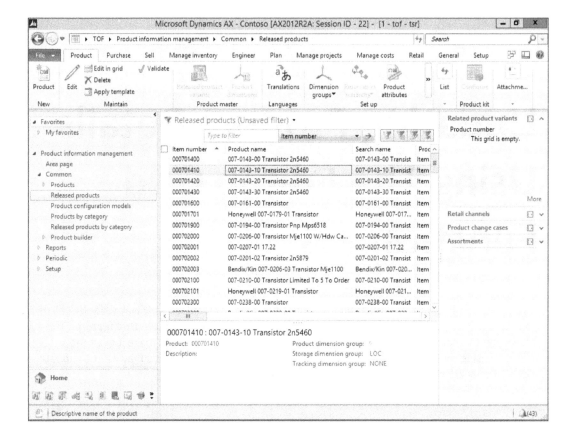

To do this, open up the **Released Product Details** list page, and click on the **Edit In Grid** button within the **Maintain** group of the **Products** ribbon bar.

Updating Product Details Using The Edit In Grid Function

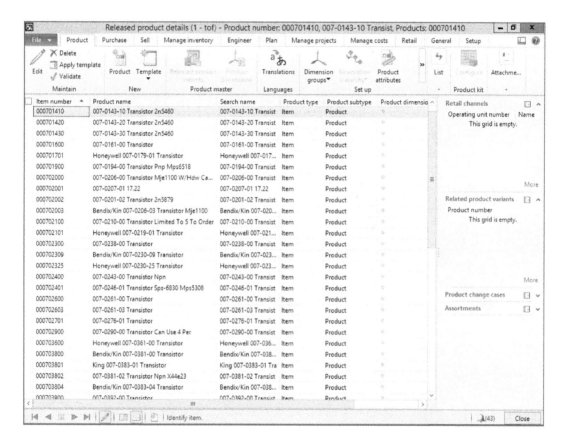

This will switch you into grid mode.

Updating Product Details Using The Edit In Grid Function

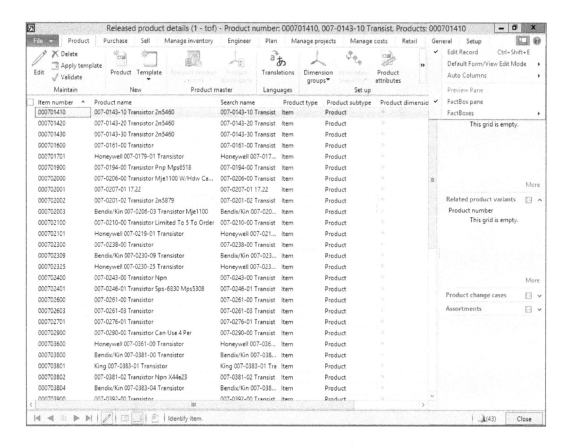

To get more real-estate, you may want to click on the **Navigation** icon in the top right hand corner of the form and uncheck the **Fact Boxes** option.

Updating Product Details Using The Edit In Grid Function

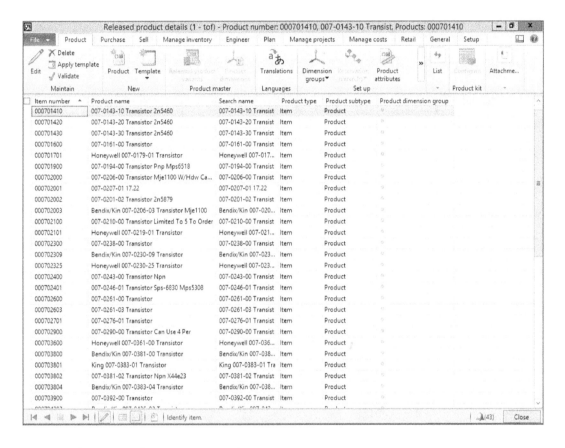

This will free you up for some power edicting.

Updating Product Details Using The Edit In Grid Function

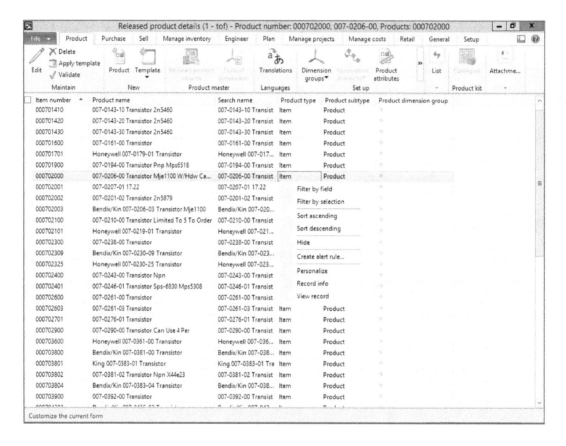

To add some additional fields that you may want to update n your products, right-mouse-click anywhere on the form and select the **Personalize** menu item.

Updating Product Details Using The Edit In Grid Function

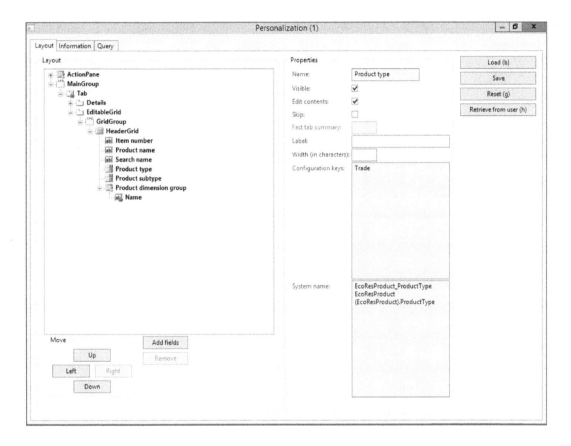

When the **Personalization** form is displayed, expand it to full screen and then click on the **Add Fields** button.

Updating Product Details Using The Edit In Grid Function

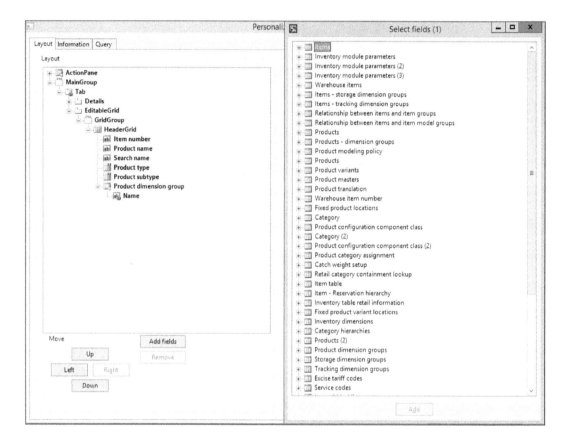

This will open up a **Select Fields** dialog box showing you all of the fields that you can add to the grid.

Tip: dock it to the right hand side of the window to get a better view.

Updating Product Details Using The Edit In Grid Function

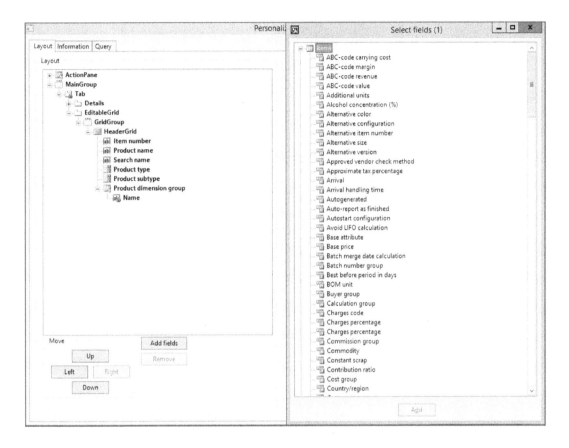

Expand out the **Items** group within the **Select Fields** dialog box to see the fields that are on the Items table.

Updating Product Details Using The Edit In Grid Function

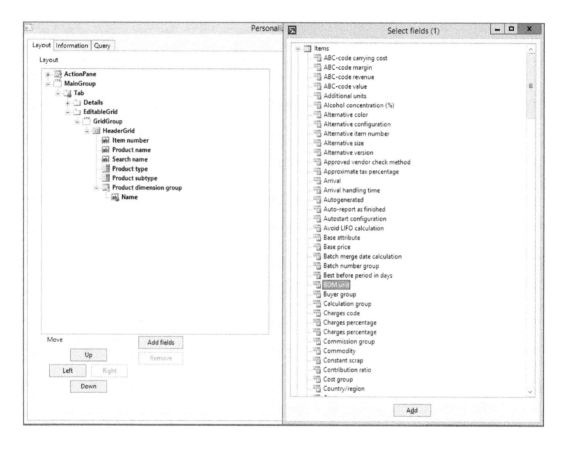

Select the **BOM unit** field and then click on the **Add** button.

Updating Product Details Using The Edit In Grid Function

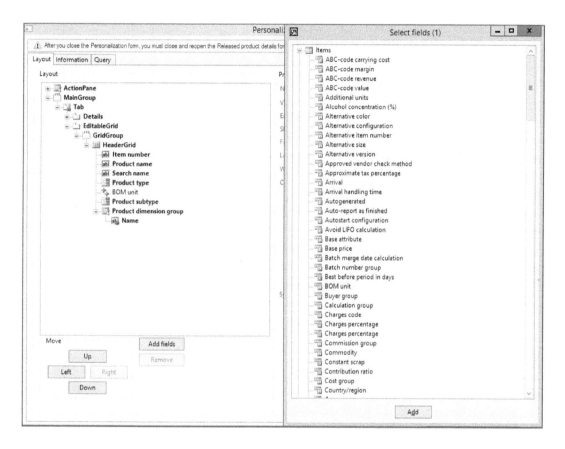

This will add the **BOM Unit** field to the grid – notice the green +'s beside the field – that tells you that it is a user added field.

Updating Product Details Using The Edit In Grid Function

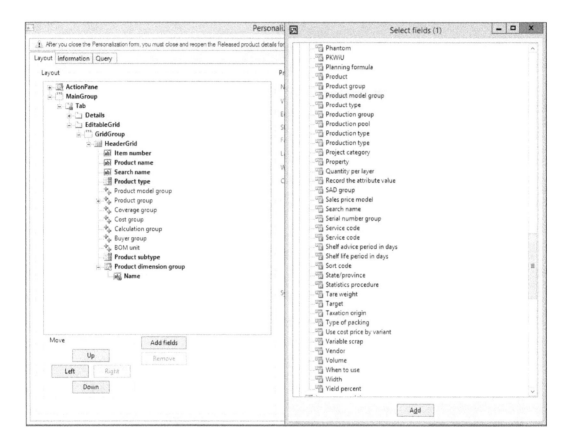

Repeat the process and add the **Buyer Group**, **Calculation Group**, **Cost Group**, **Coverage Group**, **Product Group**, and **Product Model Group** fields from the table – these are all useful fields later on.

Updating Product Details Using The Edit In Grid Function

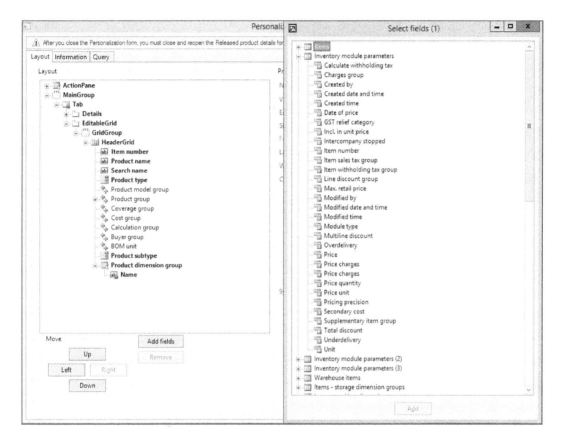

Now expand out the first **Inventory Module Parameters** field group. This contains the
Purchase Price information for the product.

Updating Product Details Using The Edit In Grid Function

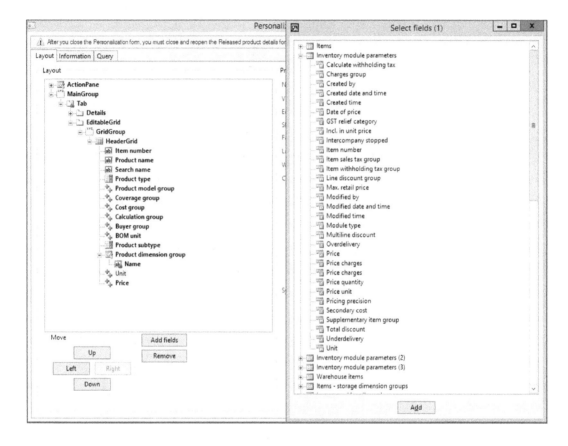

Select and add the **Price** and **Unit** fields.

Updating Product Details Using The Edit In Grid Function

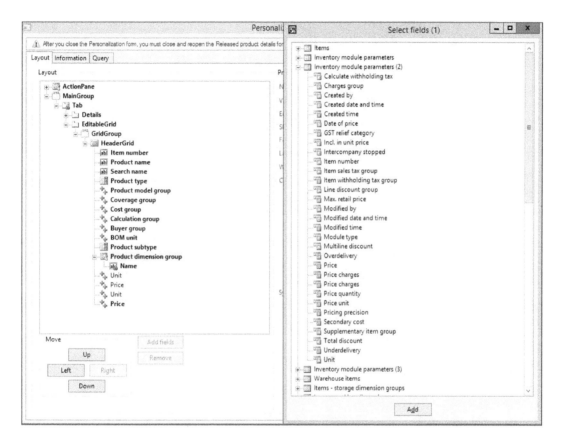

Now expand out the first **Inventory Module Parameters (2)** field group. This contains the **Cost Price** information for the product.

Select and add the **Price** and **Unit** fields.

www.dynamicsaxcompanions.com

Updating Product Details Using The Edit In Grid Function

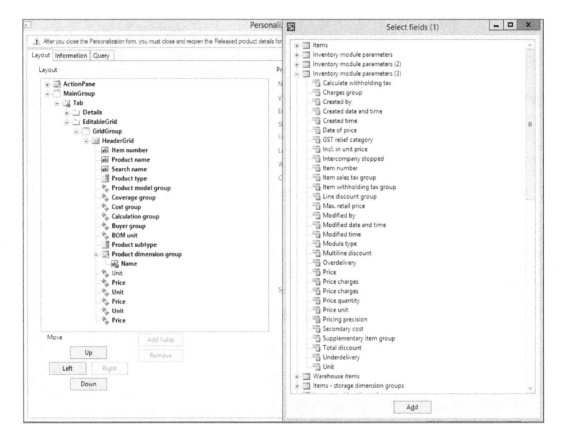

Finally expand out the first **Inventory Module Parameters (2)** field group. This contains the **Sales Price** information for the product.

Select and add the **Price** and **Unit** fields.

Then close down the **Select Fields** dialog box.

Updating Product Details Using The Edit In Grid Function

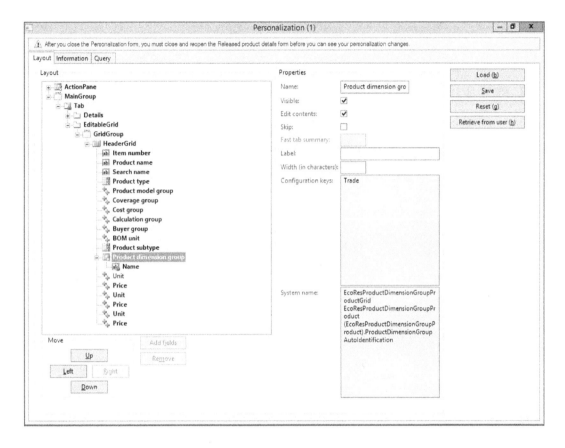

Now that you have all of the custom fields, just close down the **Personalization** form.

Updating Product Details Using The Edit In Grid Function

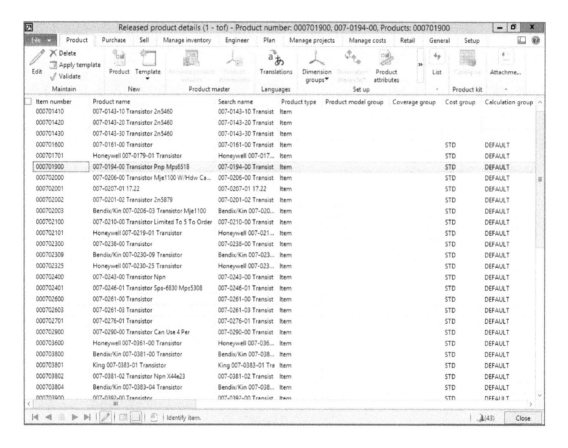

Now you will see a lot more data that you can start tweaking.

Updating Product Details Using The Edit In Grid Function

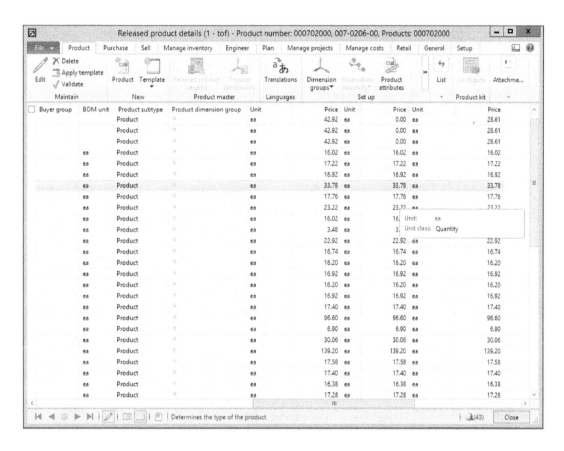

If you scroll over to the right then you will also see all of the Price and Cost details are there ready for you to edit.

Updating Product Details Using The Edit In Grid Function

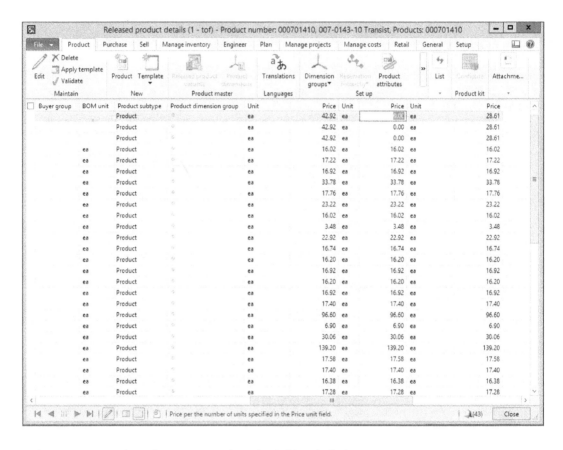

If you want to make a change, just update the field and it's done.

Updating Product Details Using The Edit In Grid Function

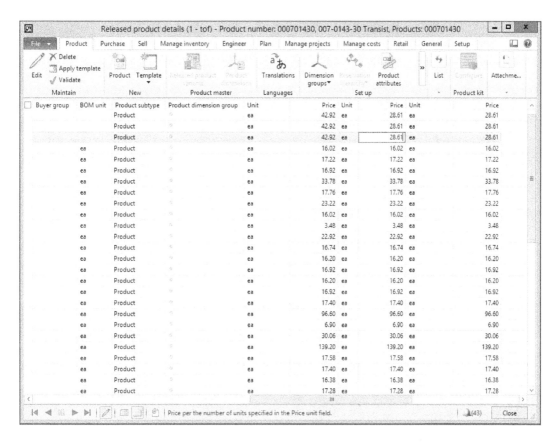

You can also update multiple fields one after the other to perform mass updates.

This is a great way to polish your data after it had been loaded in.

After you are done, you can close the form.

Using Excel To Update Product Details

If you want to perform larger updates though you may want to take advantage of the publishing feature that is available within Excel that allows you to update tables within Dynamics AX through spreadsheets.

Using Excel To Update Product Details

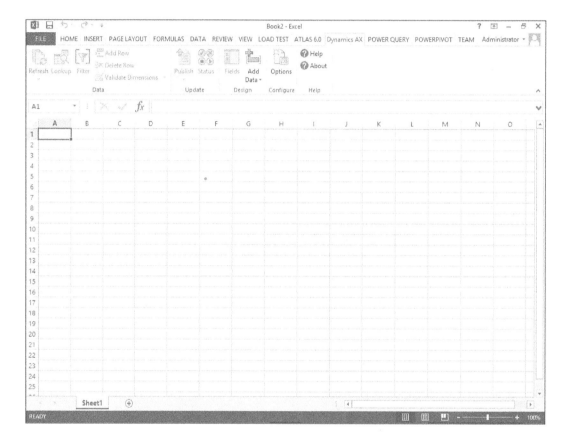

To do this, open up Excel and switch to the **Dynamics AX** ribbon bar.

Using Excel To Update Product Details

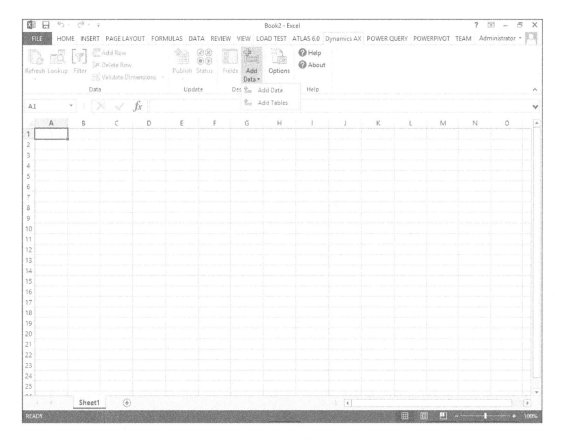

Then click on the **Add Data** button within the **Design** group of the **Dynamics AX** ribbon bar and then select the **Add Tables** menu item.

Using Excel To Update Product Details

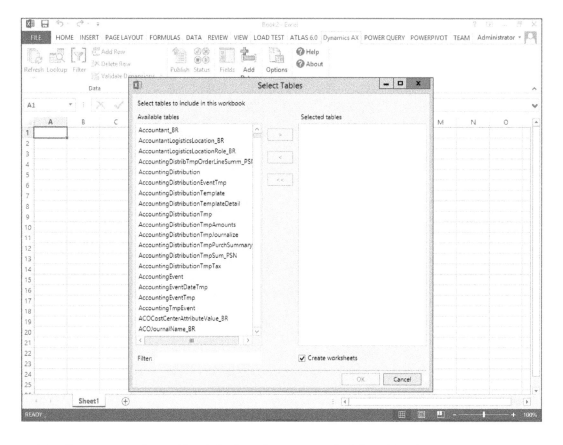

This will open up a **Select Tables** dialog box showing you all of the tables that are within **Dynamics AX**.

Using Excel To Update Product Details

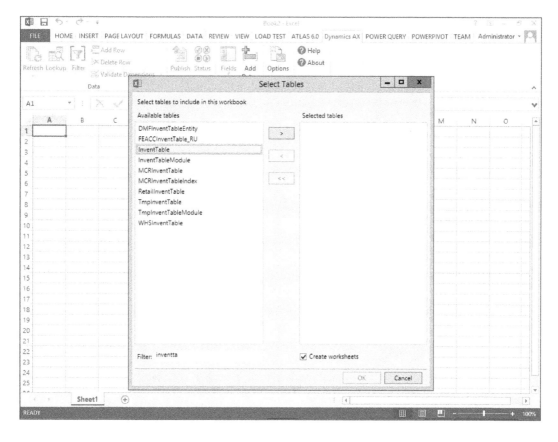

Type **InventTable** into the **Filter** field to cut down on the number of tables shown. Then select the **InventTable** table and click on the **>** button.

Using Excel To Update Product Details

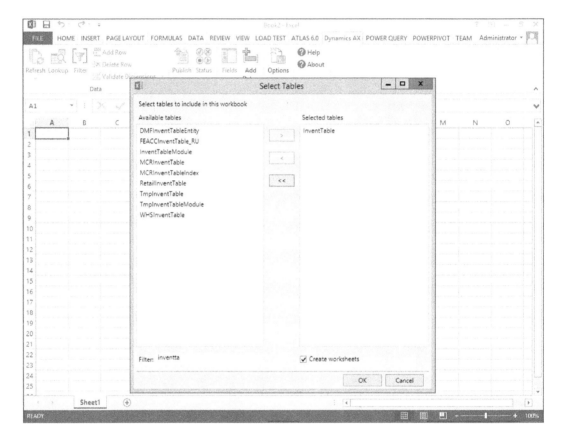

This will add the **InventTable** to the **Selected Tables** list and you can then click on the **OK** button.

Using Excel To Update Product Details

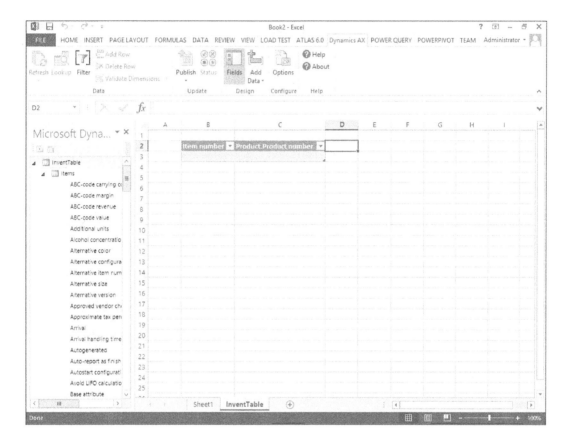

This will link your Excel worksheet with Dynamics AX and create a new worksheet for the **InventTable** showing the key fields. You will also see a field browser on the left hand side showing all of the fields that you can add to your worksheet.

Using Excel To Update Product Details

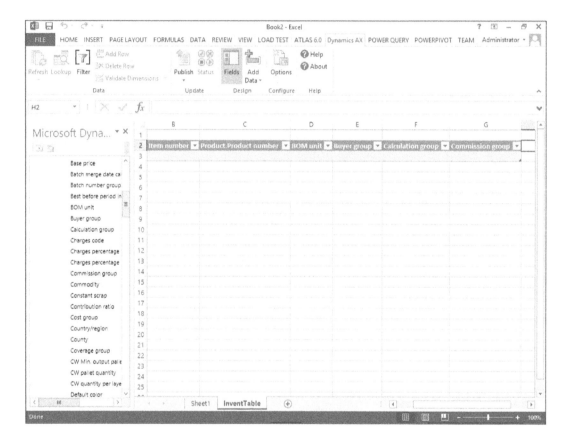

Just drag over the **BOM Unit**, **Buyer Group**, **Calculation Group**, and **Commission Group** onto the worksheet. You don't have to stop there, you can keep on adding any other field that you may want to update.

Then click on the **Fields** button within the **Design Group** of the **Dynamics AX** ribbon bar.

Note: Don't select any of the submenus – just click on the big button.

Using Excel To Update Product Details

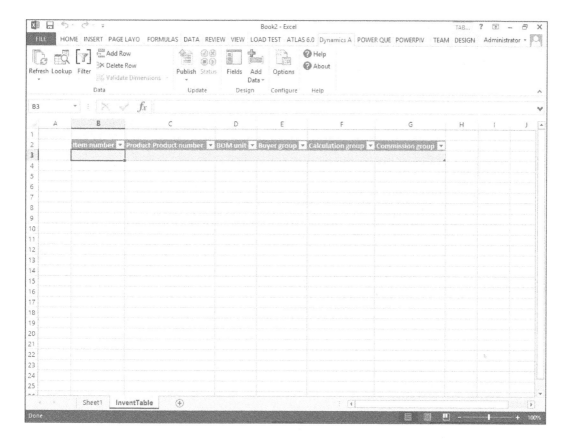

This will hide the **Field Explorer** and you will be able to click on the **Refresh** button within the **Data** group of the **Dynamics AX** ribbon bar.

Using Excel To Update Product Details

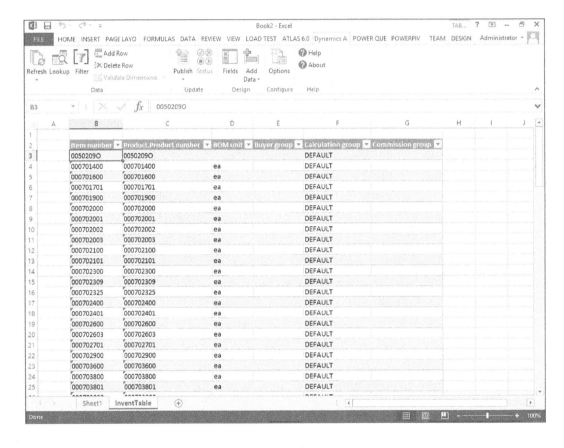

This will populate the worksheet with the live data from Dynamics AX.

Using Excel To Update Product Details

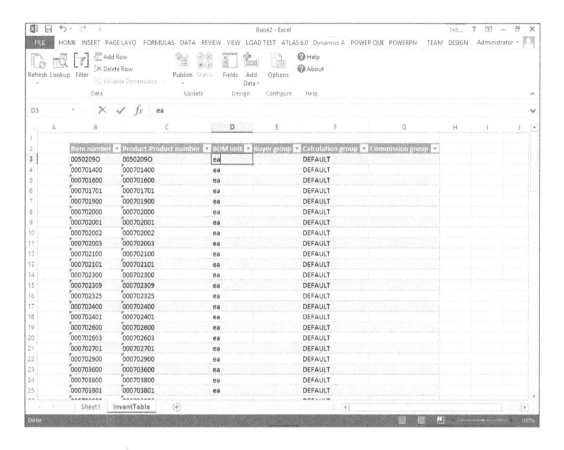

You can update any of the fields directly within the worksheet.

Using Excel To Update Product Details

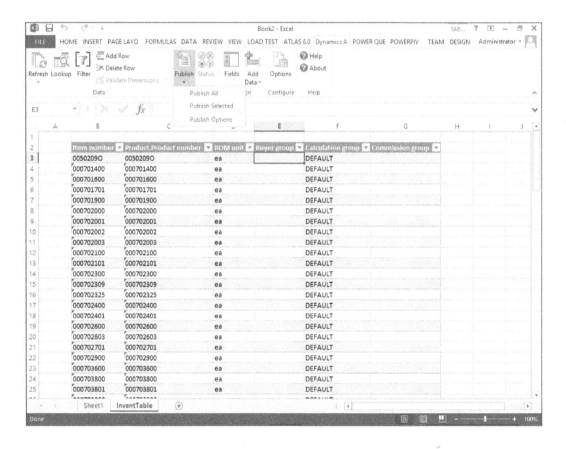

When you are done, click on the **Publish** button within the **Update** group of the **Dynamics AX** ribbon bar and select the **Publish All** submenu item.

Using Excel To Update Product Details

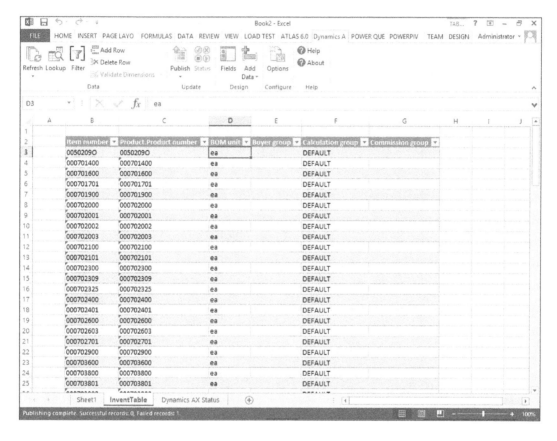

After a few seconds, Dynamics AX will make the changes and return back to the worksheet.

How easy is that?

CONFIGURING DIMENSIONAL PRODUCTS

Within Dynamics AX, a product can have a code that identifies the master product, and up to four additional **Product** Dimensions that you can use to track product variations. The default dimensions that you can track are, **Configuration**, **Size**, **Color**, and **Style**.

This allows you to simplify the product master list and still track all of the different sub-products through the dimensions. You can also track the inventory separately by product dimension, and even price out the variants differently as well.

Configuring Product Dimension Groups

The first piece that we will set up will be the **Product Dimension Groups** with all of the different types of product dimensions that we want to track.

Configuring Product Dimension Groups

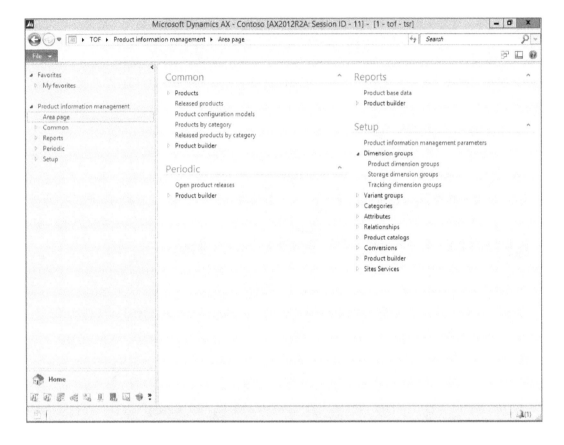

To do this, click on the **Product Dimension Groups** menu item within the **Dimension Groups** folder of the **Setup** group within the **Product Information Management** area page.

Configuring Product Dimension Groups

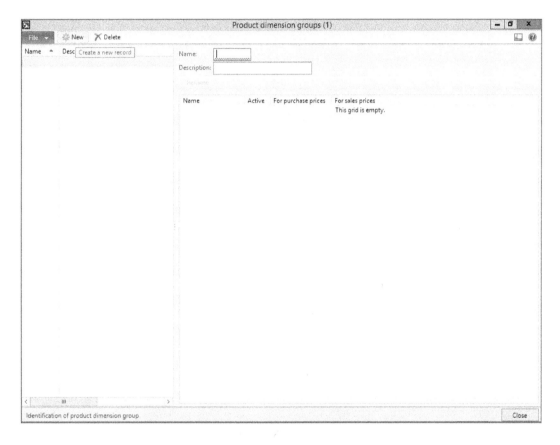

When the **Product Dimension Groups** maintenance form is displayed, click on the **New** button in the menu bar to create a new record.

Configuring Product Dimension Groups

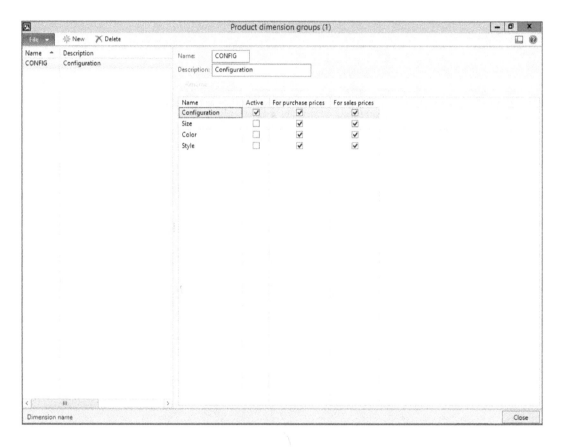

For the first record we will configure it to track product dimensions by Configuration only. So set the **Name** to **CONFIG** and the **Description** to **Configuration.**

After you have done that you will notice that the configuration options are populated with all of the available dimensions that you can add to your product, and also columns that you can use to tell the system if the dimension is active, and if it is used in sales and purchasing for pricing.

Configuring Product Dimension Groups

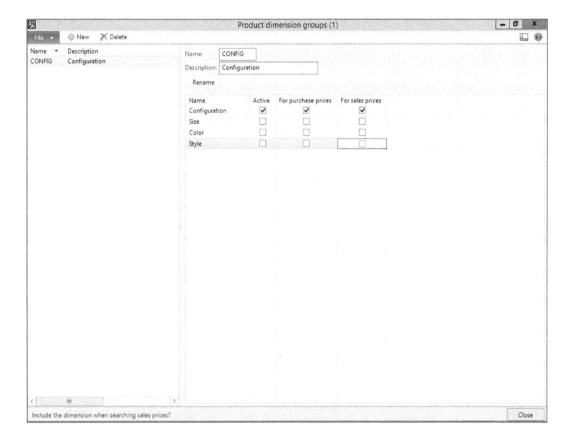

For this example we just want to track the **Configuration** dimension so we will just uncheck all of the flags that have been set on the **Size**, **Color** and **Style** dimensions for the **For Purchase Price** and **For Sales Price** columns.

Configuring Product Dimension Groups

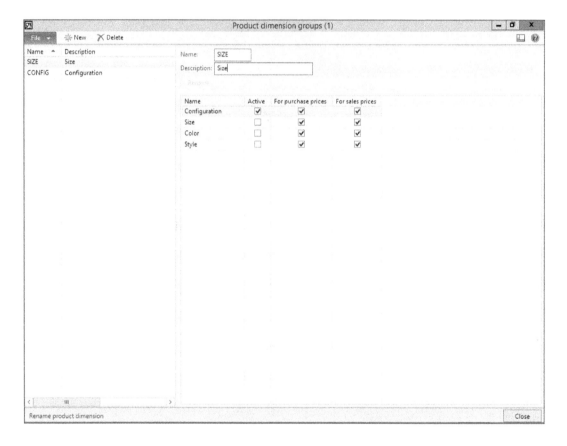

Click on the **New** button in the menu bar to create another record and set the **Name** to **SIZE** and the **Description** to **Size**.

Configuring Product Dimension Groups

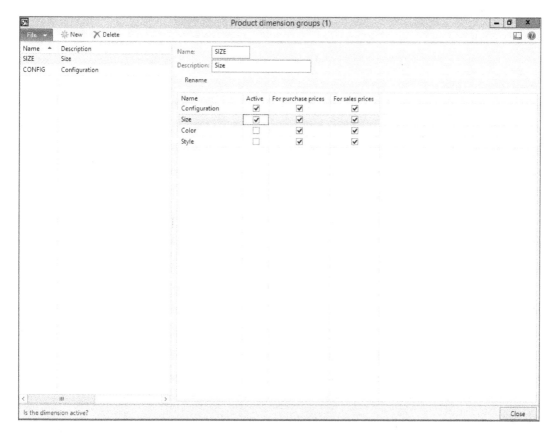

Then check the **Active** flag on the **Size** dimension to make that dimension active for this group.

Configuring Product Dimension Groups

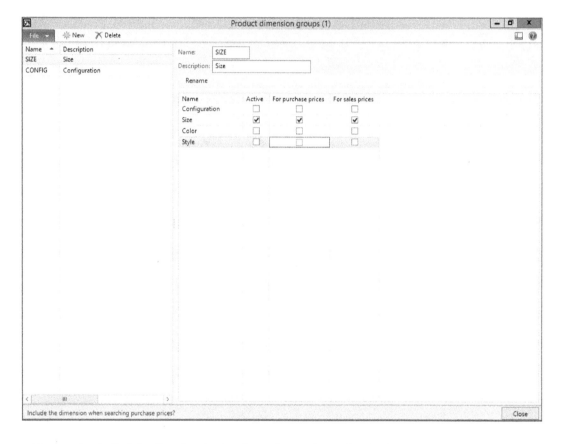

Then uncheck all of the flags for the **Configuration**, **Color** and **Style** dimensions so that only the **Size** dimension is active.

Configuring Product Dimension Groups

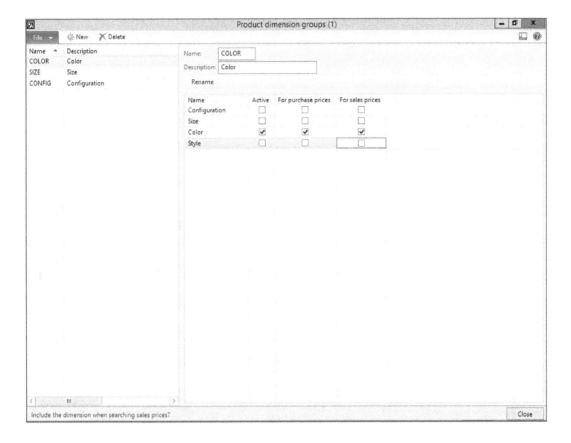

Click on the **New** button in the menu bar to create a new record. Set the **Name** to **COLOR**, the **Description** to **Color**, then check the **Active** flag on the **Color** dimension and uncheck all of the other flags for the other dimensions.

Configuring Product Dimension Groups

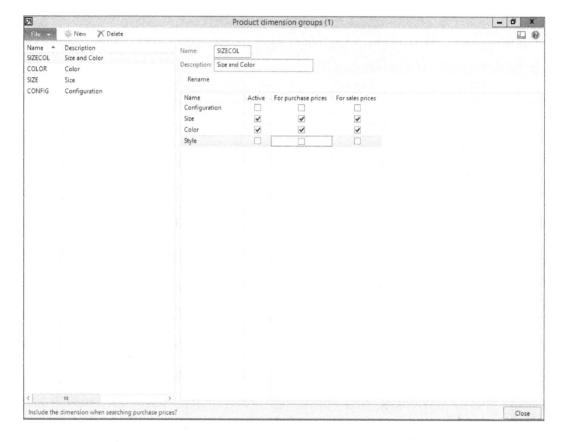

You are not limited to tracking a single product dimension against a product though. You can have multiple dimensions for products. So click on the **New** button in the menu bar to create a new record, set the **Name** to **SIZECOL** and the **Description** to **Size and Color**, and then check the **Active** flag on both the **Size** and **Color** dimensions, and uncheck all of the other dimensions pricing flags.

Configuring Product Dimension Groups

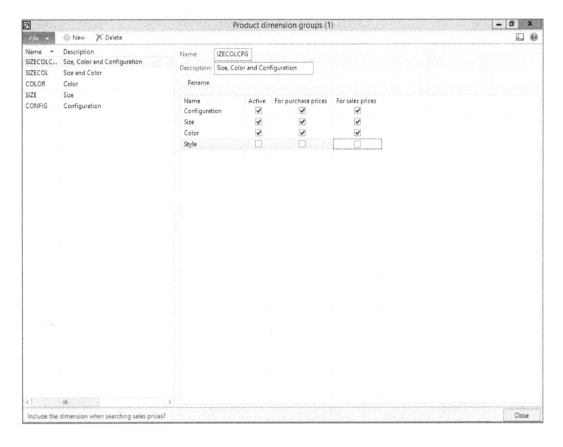

Finally we will configure one last dimension group, so click click on the **New** button in the menu bar to create a new record, set the **Name** to **SIZECOLCFG** and the **Description** to **Size, Color and Configuration**, and then check the **Active** flag on both the **Size** and **Color** dimensions, leave the flags for the Configuration dimension checked and uncheck all of the other pricing flags on the **Style** dimension.

Renaming Product Dimensions

Not everyone breaks down their products with in the same way, and the three descriptive dimensions (**Size**, **Color**, and **Style**) may not fit everyone's needs. You may want to have product variations based on model numbers, revisions, or some other dimension. If this is the case then you can use the renaming function within the **Product Dimensions** to repurpose any of the dimensions.

Renaming Product Dimensions

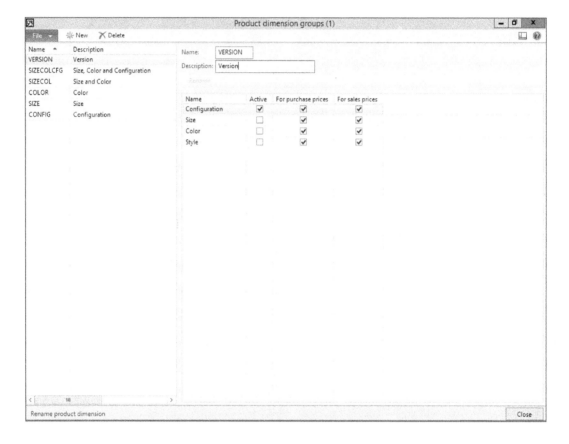

Before we do this though let's create a new Product Dimension. click on the **New** button in the menu bar to create another record and set the **Name** to **VERSION** and the **Description** to **Version**.

Renaming Product Dimensions

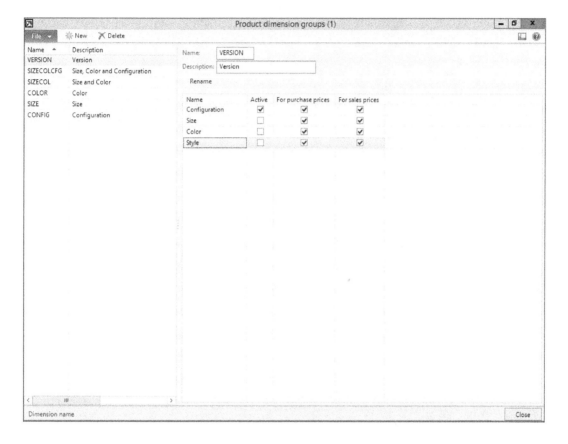

Now we will name the **Style** dimension. To do that, select the **Style** dimension and then click on the **Rename** button above the list of dimensions.

Renaming Product Dimensions

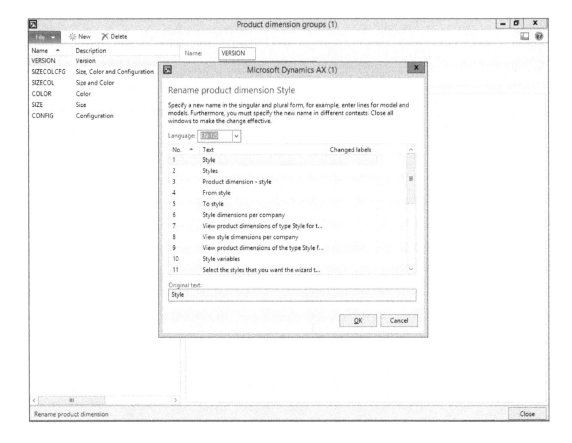

This will open up a **Rename Product Dimension Style** dialog box.

Renaming Product Dimensions

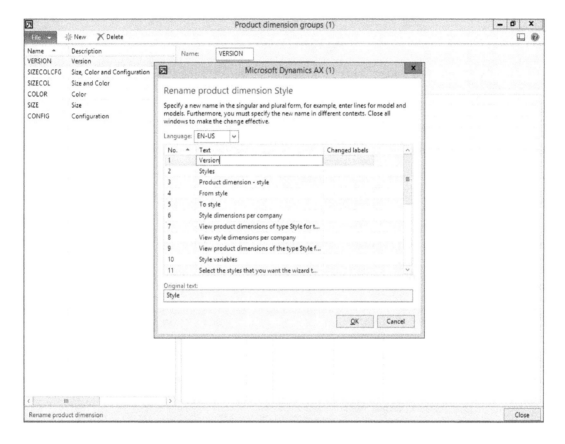

Select the first label and change the text from **Style** to **Version**.

Renaming Product Dimensions

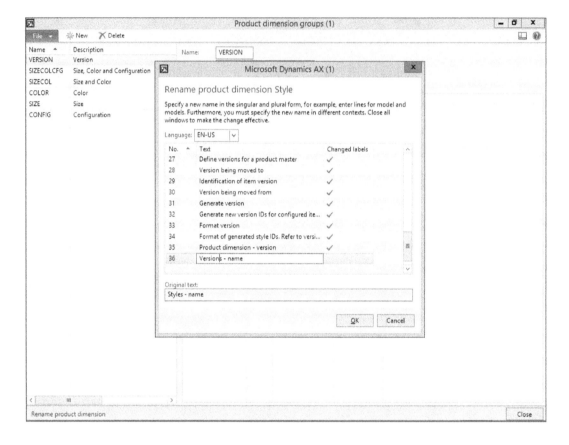

Now repeat the process for all of the other labels to make them reference **Version**.

Note: some of the labels have different forms, so you will want to be careful to keep the right description format as you do this.

Once you have updated all of the labels then click on the **OK** button to finish the update.

234

Renaming Product Dimensions

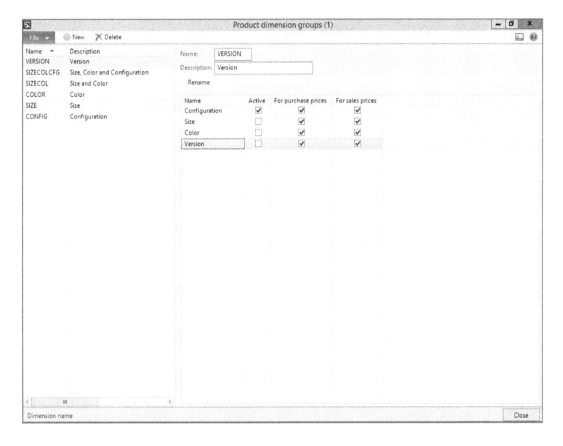

Now when you return back to the **Product Dimension Groups** maintenance form you will see
that the dimension has been changed to **Version**.

Renaming Product Dimensions

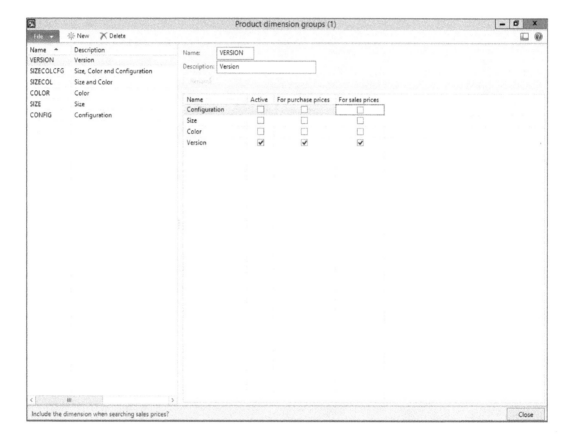

Now just uncheck all of the flags for the **Configuration**, **Size** and **Color** dimensions so that only the **Version** dimension is active.

After you are done, click on the **Close** button to exit from the form.

238

Creating A Dimensional Product

In the earlier setup we created **Dimension Groups** that defined what the valid dimension combinations were and one of them was a **Version** (or it could be though of as a model or revision) which we will use to create a product with multiple version numbers.

Creating A Dimensional Product

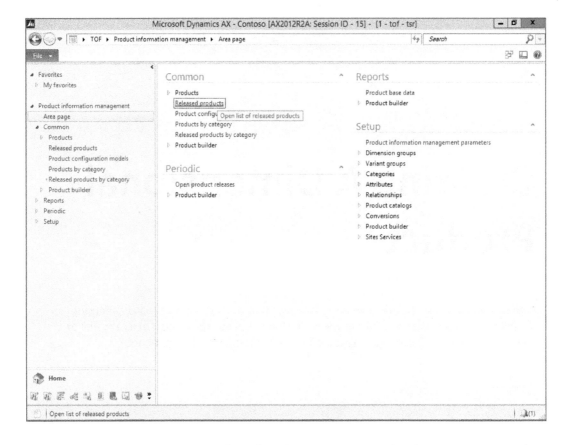

To do this, start by clicking on the **Released Products** menu item within the **Common** group of the **Product Information Management** area page.

Creating A Dimensional Product

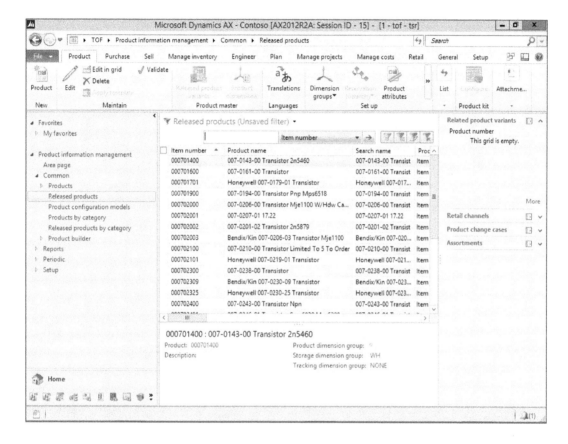

When the **Released Products** list page is displayed, click on the **Product** button within the **New** group of the **Product** ribbon bar to start creating a new product.

Creating A Dimensional Product

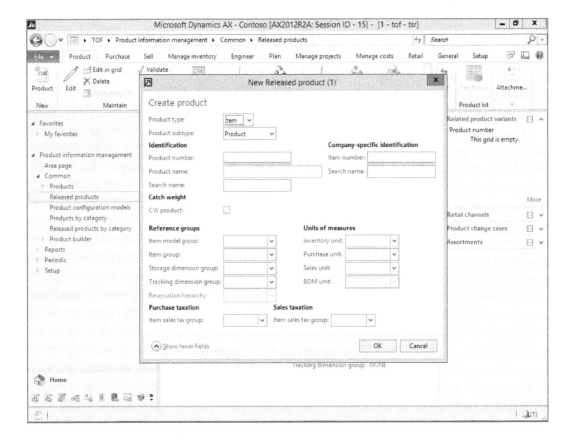

This will open up the **New Released Product** dialog box that you have seen before.

Creating A Dimensional Product

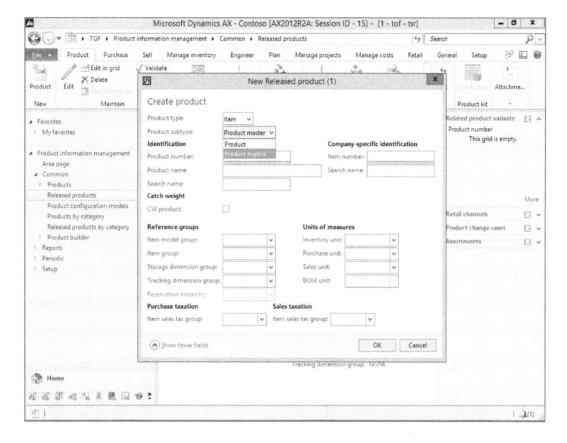

To create a dimensional product, click on the **Product Subtype** field and select the **Product Master** option.

Creating A Dimensional Product

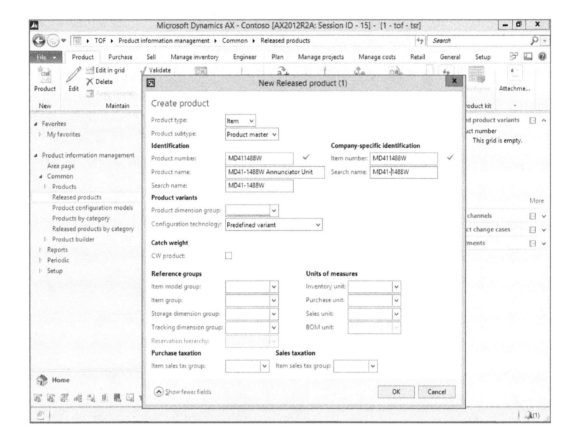

This will open up a new field group that you haven't seen yet for **Product Variants.** Before we get to that though set the **Product Number** to **MD411488W** and the **Product Name** to **MD41-1488W Annunciator Unit.**

Creating A Dimensional Product

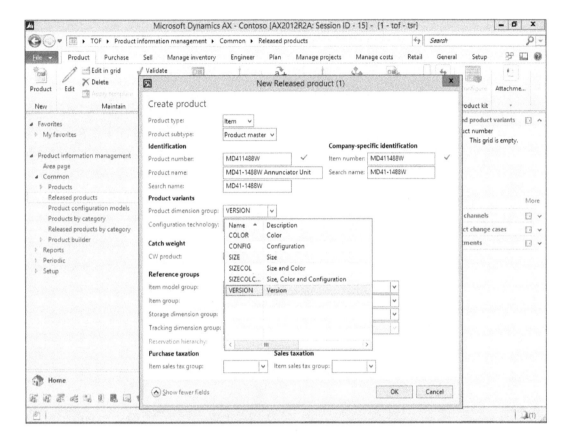

Then click on the **Product Dimension Group** dropdown list and you will see all of the **Dimension Groups** that you configured earlier on. Select the **Version** record.

Creating A Dimensional Product

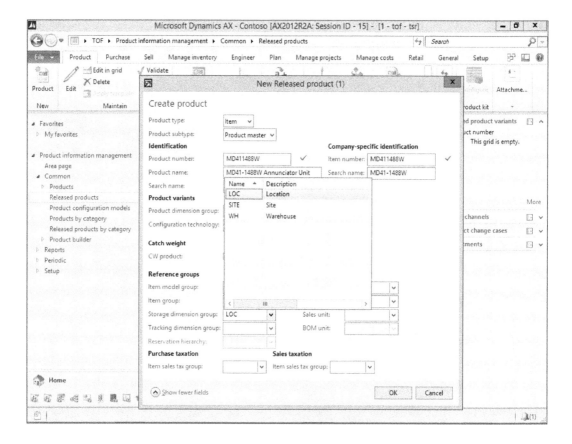

Now click on the **Storage Dimension** field and select the **LOC** record.

Creating A Dimensional Product

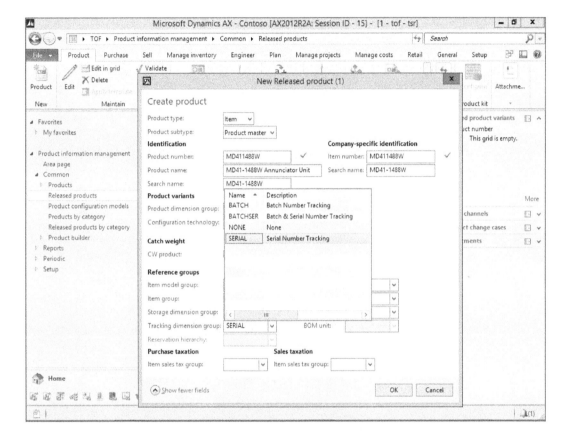

And click on the **Tracking Dimension** dropdown list and select the **Serial Number** record (because we want to track the serial number of every one of these items).

Creating A Dimensional Product

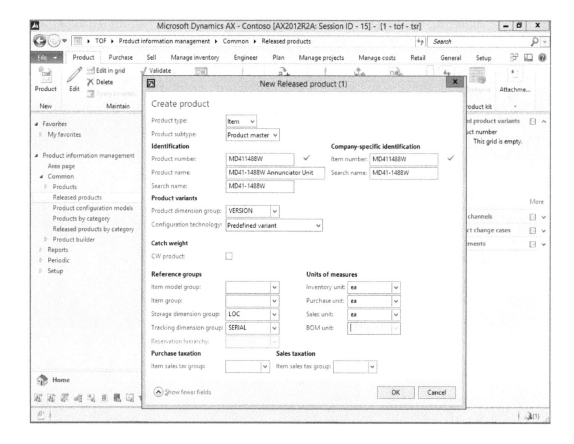

Then set the **Inventory Unit**, **Purchase Unit**, and **Sales Unit** to **ea.**

After you have done that, click on the **OK** button to create the product.

Creating A Dimensional Product

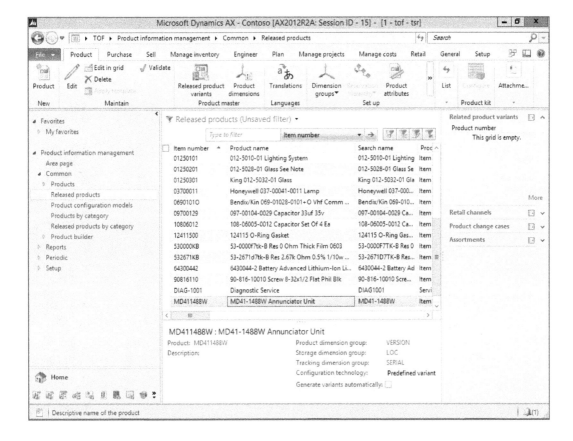

When you return to the **Released Products** list page you will see your new product.

Creating A Dimensional Product

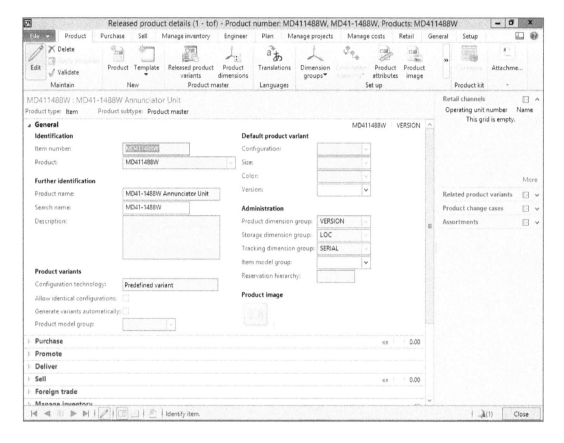

If you open up the product then you will be able to update all of the details like you did before.

Specifying Product Dimensions

One of the special features of the **Dimensional Product** is that is has dimensions, so the next step is to define all of the valid dimensions for the product.

Specifying Product Dimensions

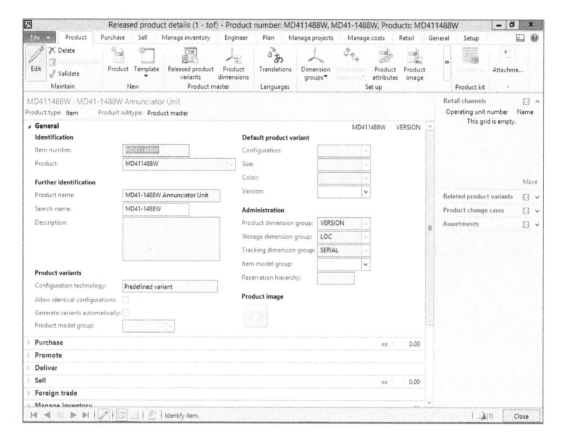

To do this, return back to the **Released Product** detail page, and you will notice that a couple of new buttons are enabled within the **Product Master** group of the **Product** ribbon bar. Start off by clicking on the **Product Dimensions** button.

Specifying Product Dimensions

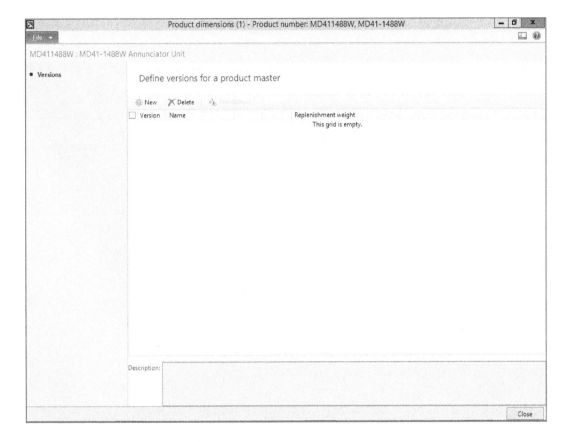

This will open up the **Product Dimensions** maintenance form, and all of the dimensions that are enabled within the **Dimension Group** will be displayed on the left hand side. In this case there is only one – which is the **Version**.

Specifying Product Dimensions

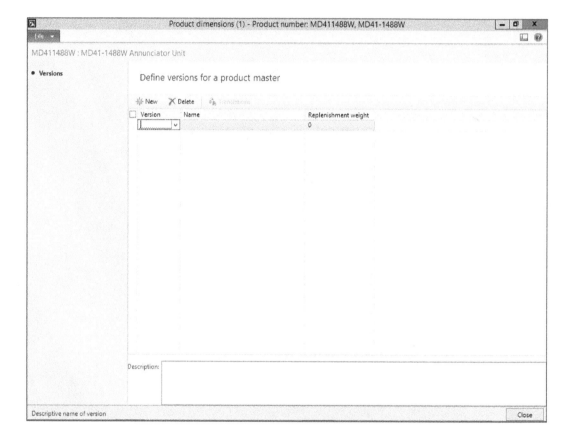

To add a new valid **Version Dimension** click on the **New** button in the menu bar of the dimension grid.

Specifying Product Dimensions

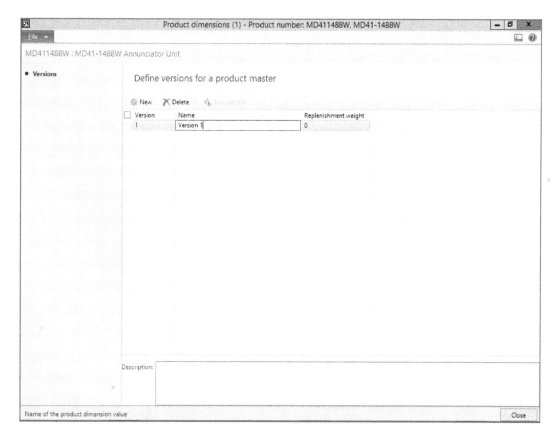

Set the **Version** to **1** and the **Name** to **Version 1**.

Specifying Product Dimensions

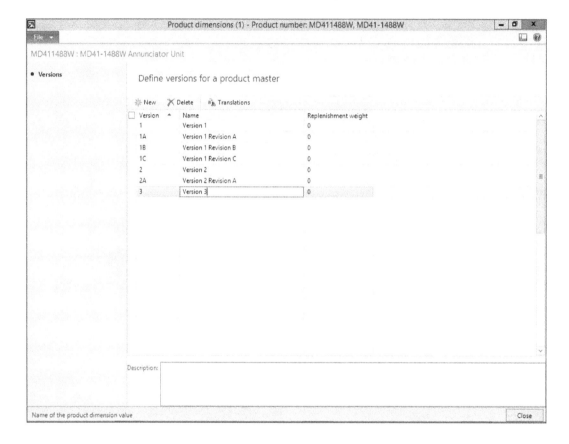

Repeat the process a few more times for the other versions that are available for the product, and when you are done, click on the **Close** button.

Releasing Product Variants

There is one last step that we need to perform, and that is to release the valid **Dimension Variants** to the product. What this means is that we are going to choose what variations of dimensions are allowed to be used against a product. Just because the product has a dimension, it doesn't mean that we need to use it.

Releasing Product Variants

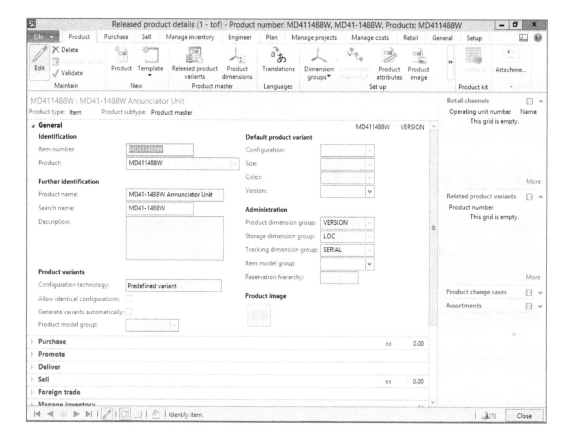

To do this, return to the **Released Product** and click on the **Released Product Variants** button within the **Product Master** group of the **Product** ribbon bar.

Releasing Product Variants

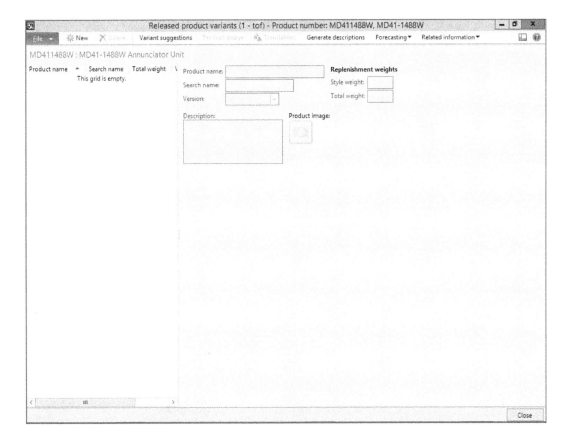

This will open up a new maintenance form for the **Released Product Variants**. We can create the valid variations by hand if we want by clicking on the **New** button, although an easier way is to have Dynamics AX suggest the variants for us. To do this, click on the **Variant Suggestions** button in the menu bar.

Releasing Product Variants

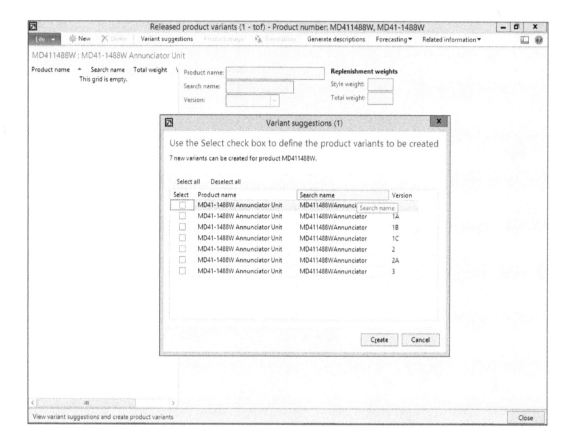

This will open up a dialog box showing us all of the possible combinations of **Dimensions** for this product.

Releasing Product Variants

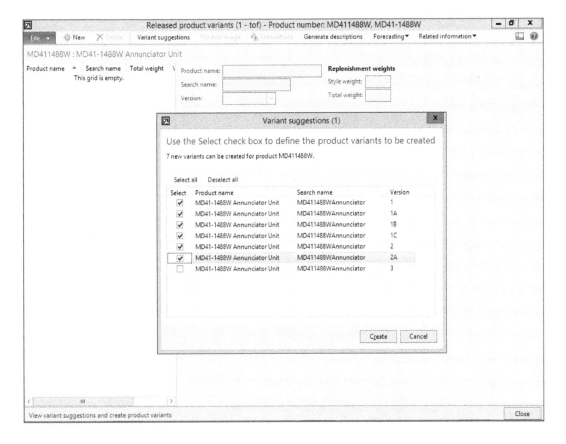

All you need to do is select the variants that you want to use for the product and click on the **Create** button.

Releasing Product Variants

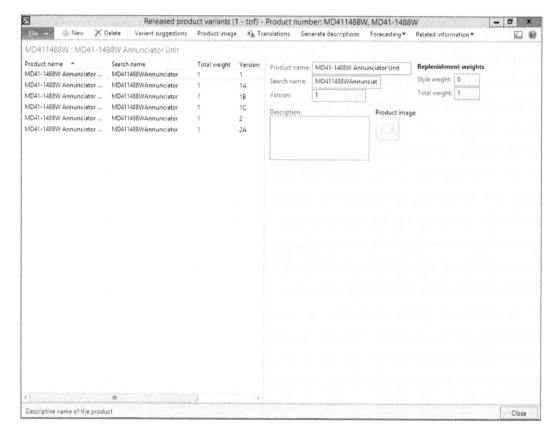

Now they will all be loaded for you in the **Released Product Variants** maintenance form.

Releasing Product Variants

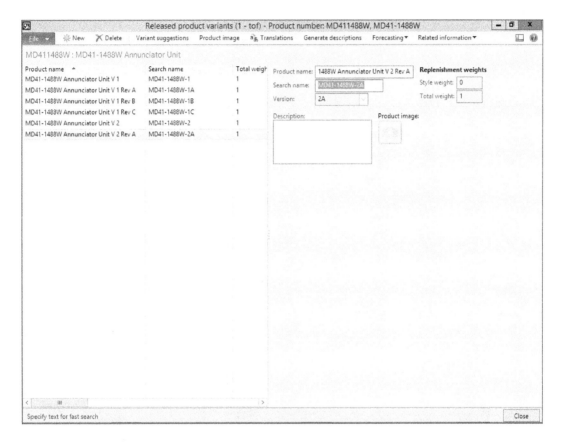

If you want you can change the suggested name for each of the **Variants**.

When you are done, just click on the **Close** button to exit from the form.

Releasing Product Variants

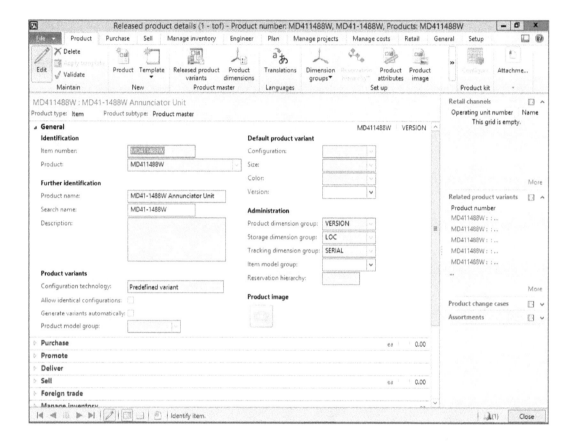

When you return back to the **Released Product** maintenance form, look over to the right hand side and you will see that the **Released Product Variants** fact box now lists all of the variants for you.

Enabling Costing By Variant

Product costs are usually pretty simple, because each product has only one cost, but when you add in product variants this may not be the case. Different sizes of products may cost more or less and in our example, different versions or revisions of a product may have different costs. So there is a choice that you can make within you setup as to if costs are different by variant or not.

If they are not then there is nothing that you need to do, but if you do have different costs by product variant then you will want to make a small change.

Enabling Costing By Variant

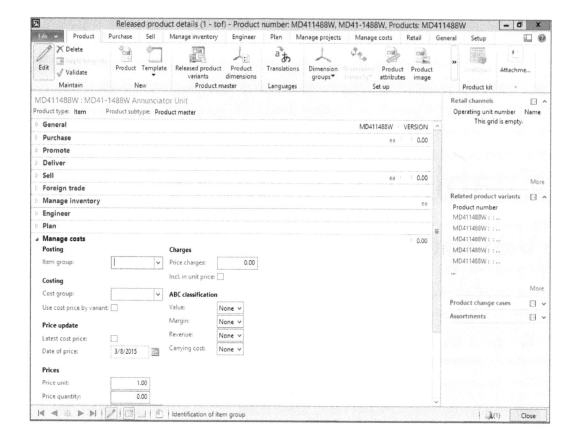

To do this, just open up your **Released Product Details** and expand out the **Manage Costs** tab group.

Enabling Costing By Variant

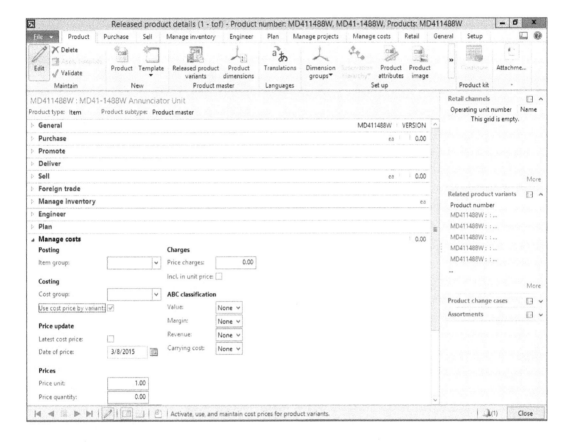

All you need to do is set the **Use Cost Price by Variant** flag. You are done and you can click on the **Close** button to exit from the form.

CONFIGURING PRODUCT CATEGORIES AND ATTRIBUTES

If you have any additional information or properties that you want to track against a product, you don't have to resort to adding fields to the table and then modifying the forms so that you have a place to store it. You can take advantage of the product attributes feature within Dynamics AX to add an unlimited number of additional pieces of data. You don't even have to have the same attributes for all of the products, by using the Product Categories, you can assign specific groups of attributes to different groups of products.

Configuring Attribute Types

The first step in configuring Product Attributes is to define the different **Attribute Types** that you are allowed to use. These control the type of values that are allowed to be recorded against the attributes and also the units of measure that are associated with the attributes as well. They are also re-usable over multiple attributes so they give you a little bit of consistency when you set up your Attribute structures.

Configuring Attribute Types

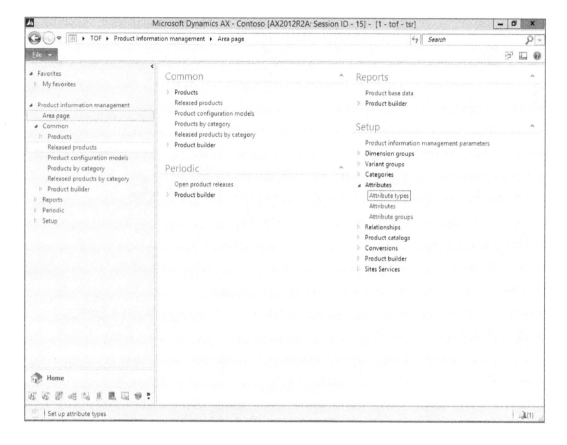

To do this, click on the **Attribute Types** menu item within the **Attributes** folder of the **Setup** group within the **Product Information Management** area page.

Configuring Attribute Types

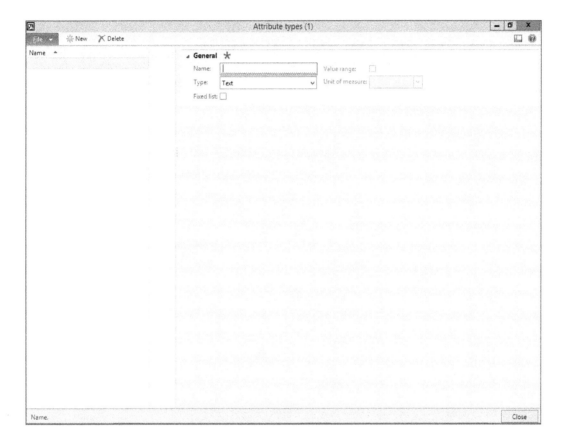

When the **Attribute Types** maintenance form is displayed, click on the **New** button in the menu bar to create a new record.

Configuring Attribute Types

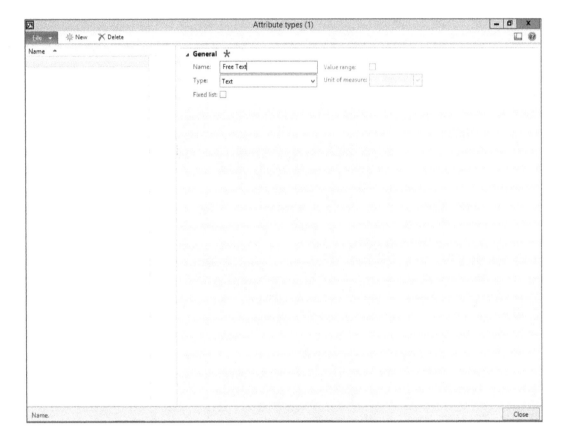

Let's start by setting up a general **Attribute Type** by setting the **Name** to **Free Text** and the **Type** to **Text**.

Configuring Attribute Types

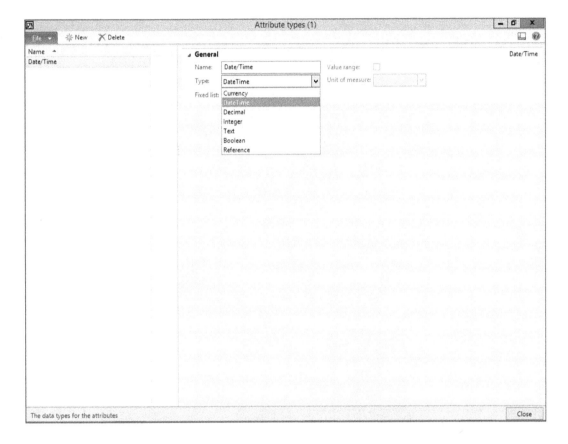

Next we will create an attribute for date and time, so click on the **New** button in the menu bar to create a new record, set the **Name** to **Date/Time** and click on the **Type** dropdown list and select the **DateTime** item.

Configuring Attribute Types

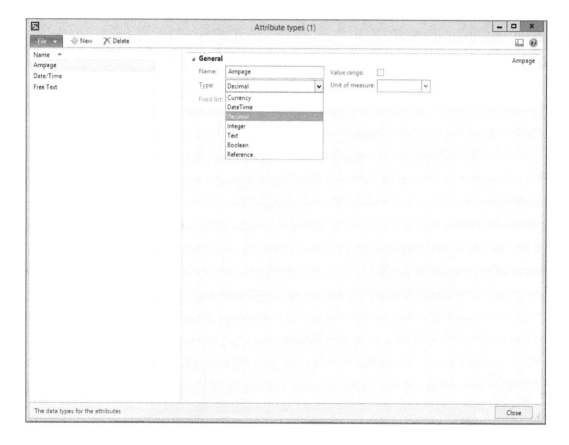

Next we will set up a Attribute Type for something a little less generic. Click on the **New** button in the menu bar to create a new record and then set the **Name** to **Ampage**. Then click on **Type** fields dropdown list and select the **Decimal** value.

Configuring Attribute Types

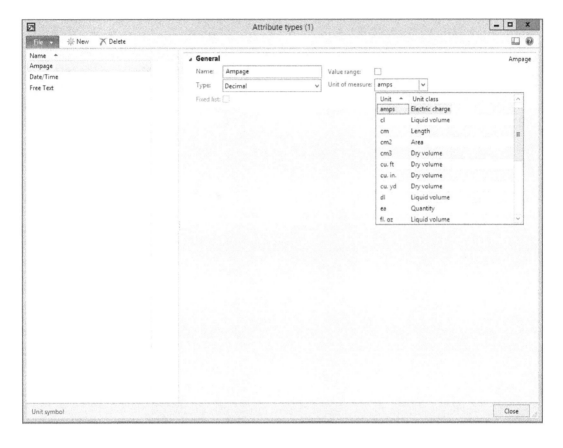

For this **Attribute Type** we want to also click on the **Unit Of Measure** dropdown list and select **amps**.

Configuring Attribute Types

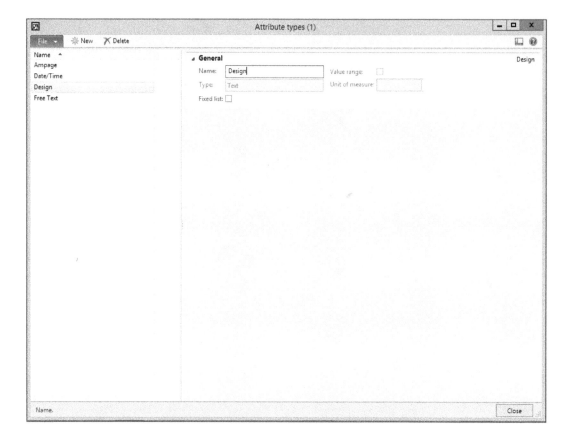

We will create one last **Attribute Type** which will have a list of valid values. To do this click on the **New** button in the menu bar to create a new record, and set the **Name** to **Design**.

Configuring Attribute Types

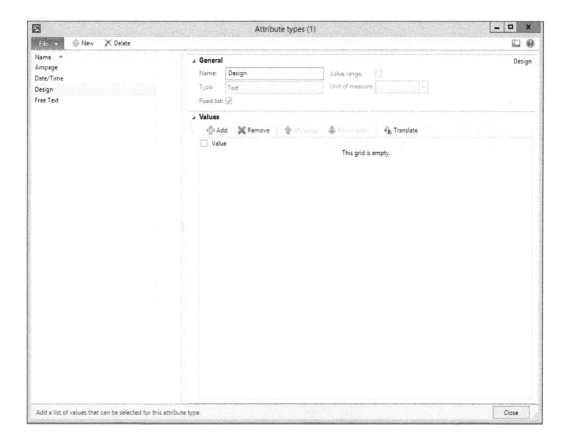

Next check the **Fixed List** flag on the record.

Configuring Attribute Types

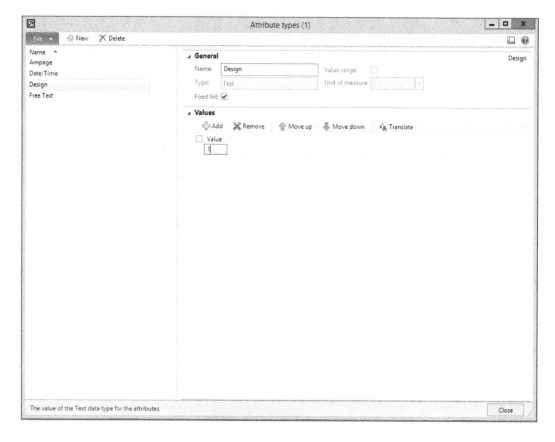

This will allow you to click on the **Add** button in the **Values** tab group and create a new value record.

Configuring Attribute Types

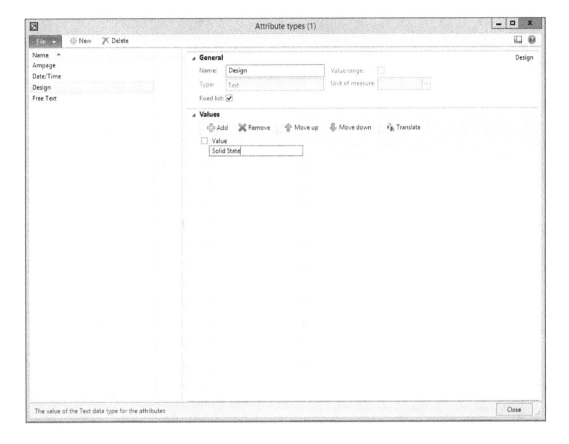

Set the **Value** to **Solid State**.

Configuring Attribute Types

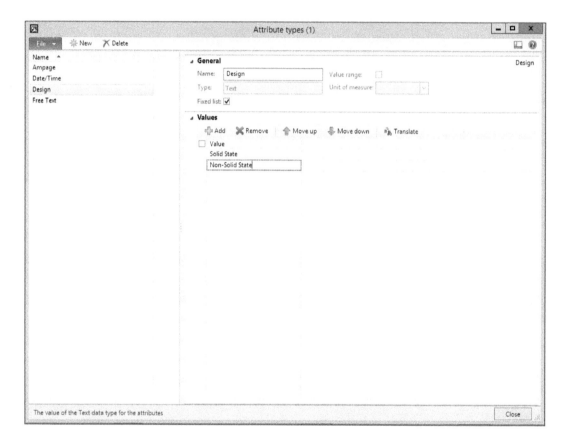

Click on the **Add** button again to add a new **Attribute Type Value** and set the **Value** to **Non-Solid-State**.

After you have done that you can click on the **Close** button and exit from the form.

Configuring Attributes

Now that we have some **Attribute Types** defined we can start using them to define some **Attributes** that we want to track against our products.

Configuring Attributes

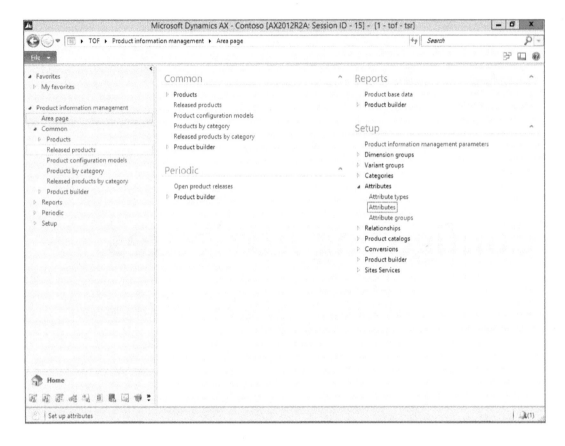

To do this, click on the **Attributes** menu item within the **Attributes** folder of the **Setup** group within the **Product Information Management** area page.

Configuring Attributes

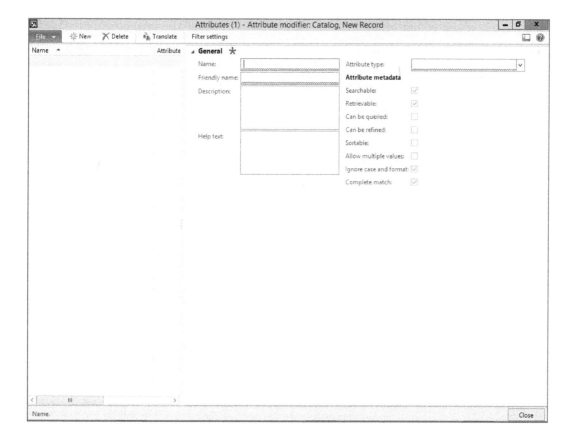

When the **Attributes** maintenance form is displayed, click on the **New** button in the menu bar to create a new record.

Configuring Attributes

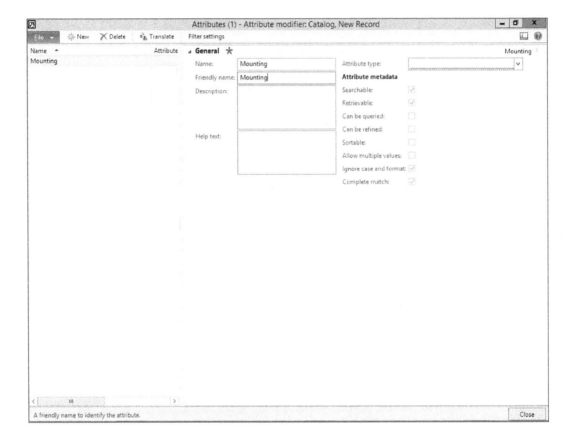

Set the **Name** and **Friendly Name** to **Mounting.**

Configuring Attributes

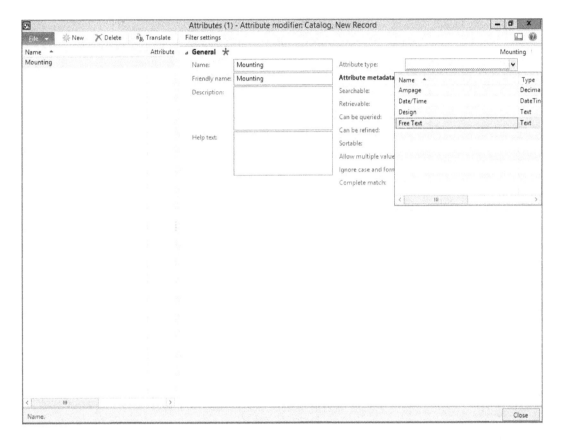

Then click on the **Attribute Type** dropdown list and select the **Free Text** record to indicate that we can type anything we like into this attribute.

Configuring Attributes

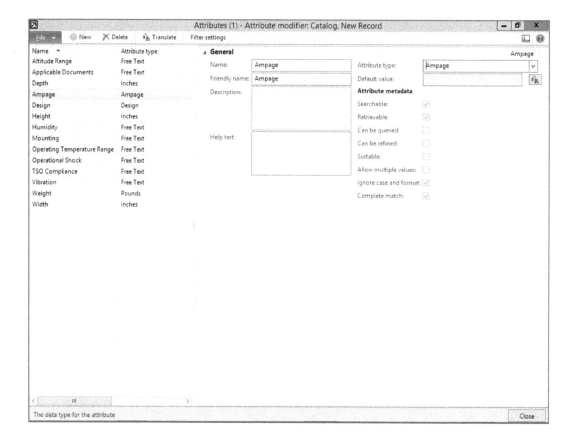

After you have done that, repeat the process to add all of the other dimensions that you want to track against the product. Notice that you can re-use the **Attribute Types** over as many of the **Attributes** that you want to.

After you are done, click on the **Close** button to exit from the form.

Configuring Attribute Groups

Once you have your **Attributes** defined then you can create **Attribute Groups** which will allow you to group common attributes together and also make it easier for you at assign those groups of attributes to products.

Configuring Attribute Groups

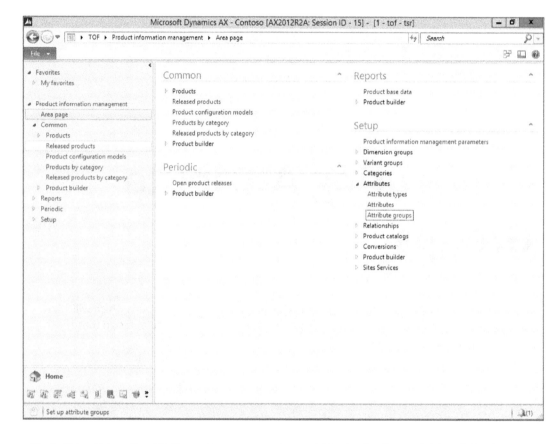

To do this, click on the **Attribute Groups** menu item within the **Attributes** folder of the **Setup** group within the **Product Information Management** area page.

daxc

Configuring Attribute Groups

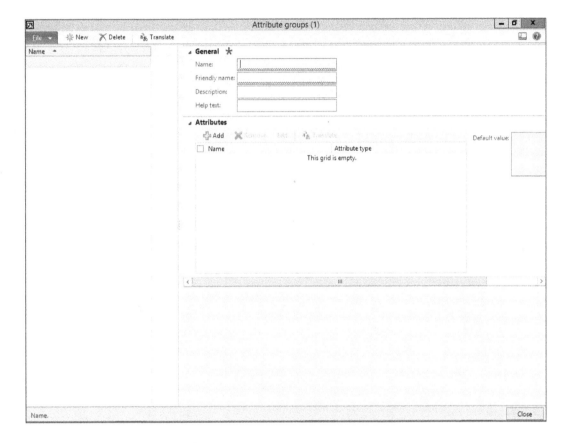

When the **Attribute Groups** maintenance form is displayed, click on the **New** button in the menu bar to create a new record.

Configuring Attribute Groups

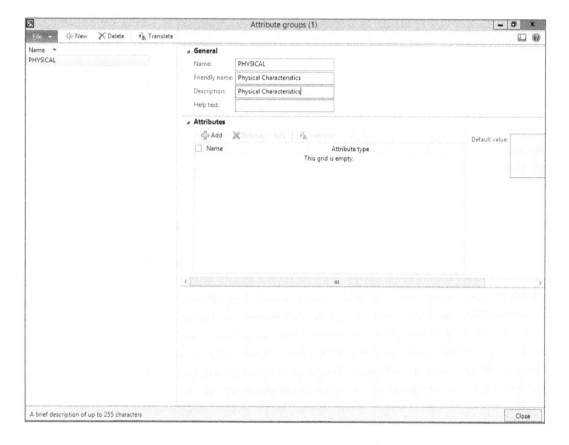

Set the **Name** to **PHYSICAL** and the **Friendly Name** and **Description** to **Physical Characteristics**.

Then click on the **Add** button within the **Attributes** tab group.

Configuring Attribute Groups

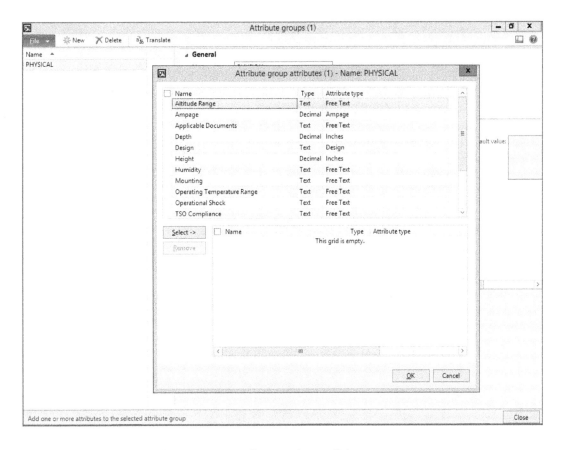

This will open up an **Attribute Group Attributes** selector dialog.

Configuring Attribute Groups

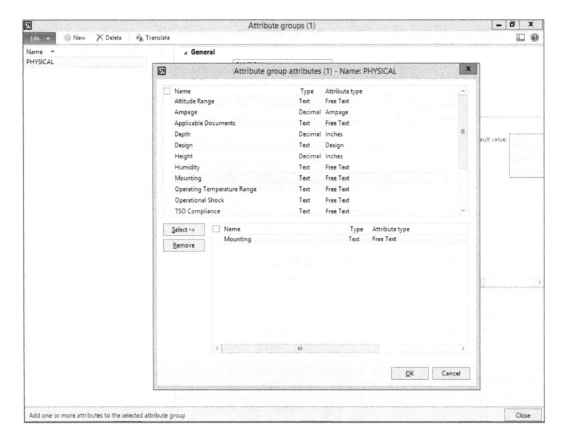

All you need to do is select the **Attribute (Mounting** for example) that you want to add to the group, and click on the **Select** button. This will add it to the selected attribute list.

Configuring Attribute Groups

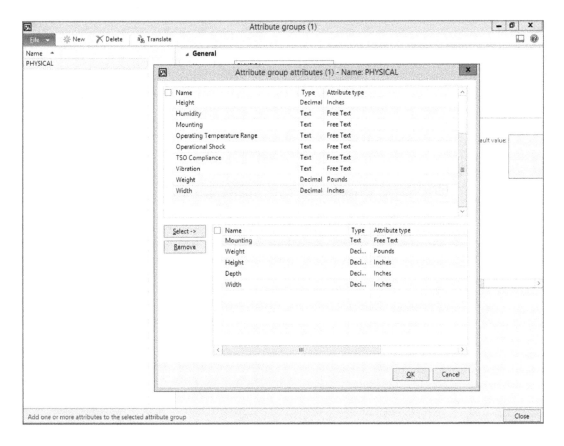

You can repeat the process for all of the other **Attributes** that you want to add to the group. i.e. **Weight, Height, Depth**, and **Width**.

When you are done, just click on the **Close** button to exit out of the form.

Configuring Attribute Groups

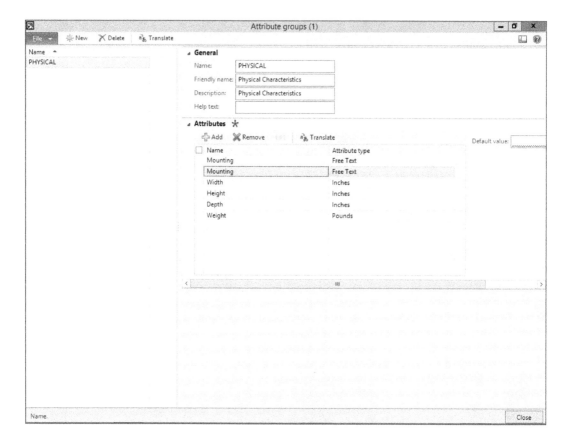

When you return back to the **Attribute Groups** maintenance form you will see that the **Attributes** are now set up.

Configuring Attribute Groups

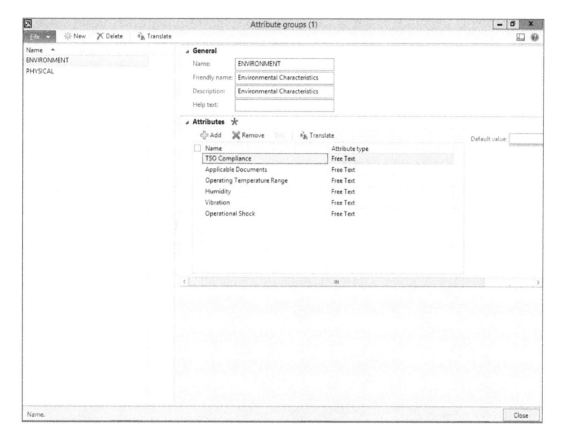

Click on the **New** button in the menu bar and create a new record. Set the **Name** to **ENVIRONMENT**, and the **Friendly Name** and **Description** to **Environmental Characteristics**.

Then click the **Add** button and select all of the associated **Attributes** to it.

Configuring Attribute Groups

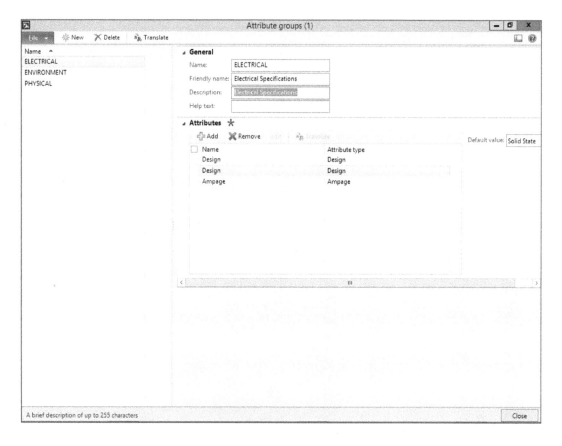

Set up one last **Attribute Group** by clicking on the **New** button in the menu bar and create a new record. Set the **Name** to **ELSECTRICAL**, and the **Friendly Name** and **Description** to **Electrical Specifications**.

Then click the **Add** button and select all of the associated **Attributes** to it.

When you are done, click on the **Close** button to exit from the form.

Configuring Category Hierarchies

Now that the **Attributes** are configured we can start associating them to our products. You don't do that through the product itself, you do it by creating product **Category Hierarchies** that group the products together and then assigning the **Attribute Groups** to them. So the next step in the process is to create some **Category Hierarchies**.

Configuring Category Hierarchies

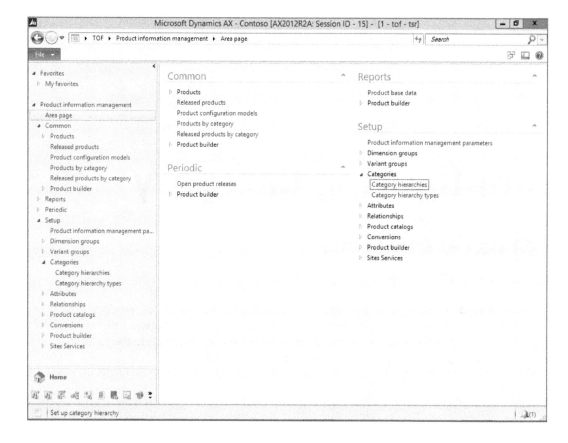

To do this, click on the **Category Hierarchies** menu item within the **Categories** folder of the **Setup** group within the **Product Information Management** area page.

Configuring Category Hierarchies

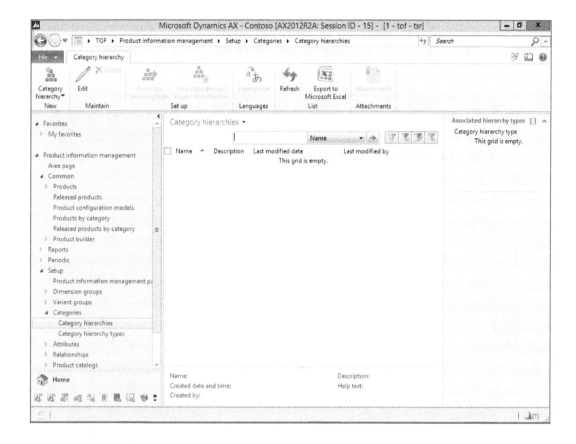

This will open up the **Category Hierarchies** list page.

Configuring Category Hierarchies

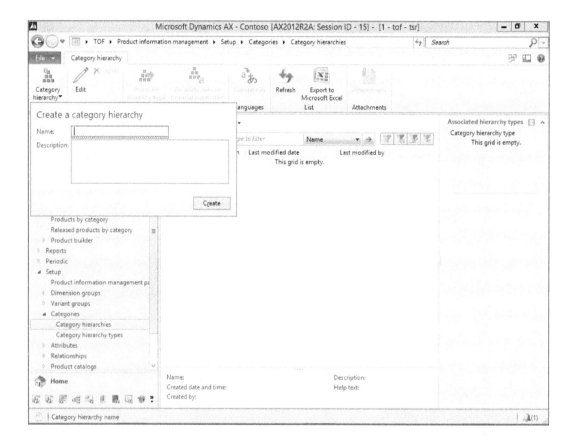

Click on the **Category Hierarchy** button within the **New** group of the **Category Hierarchy** ribbon bar which will open up a quick add window.

Configuring Category Hierarchies

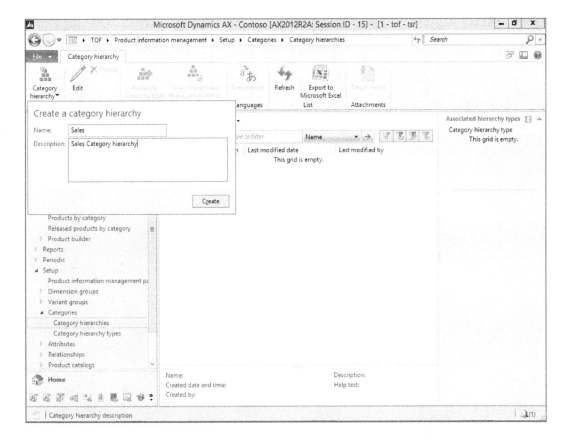

Set the **Name** to **Sales** and the **Description** to **Sales Category Description**. Then click on the **Create** button.

Configuring Category Hierarchies

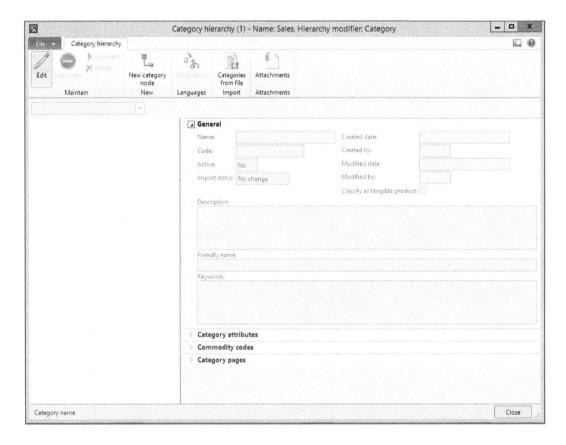

This will open up a new **Category Hierarchy** maintenance form.

Configuring Category Hierarchies

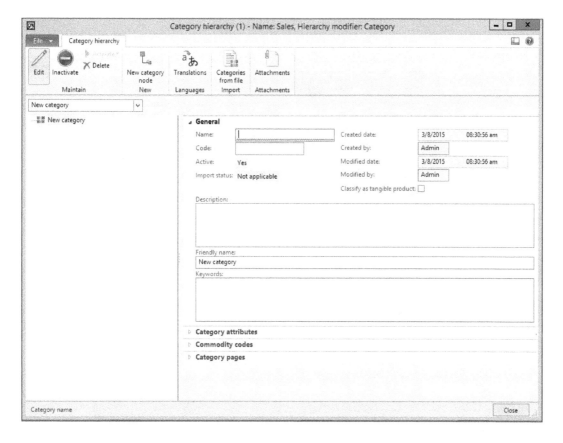

To start building your hierarchy, click on the **New Category Node** button within the **New** group of the **Category Hierarchy** ribbon bar.

Configuring Category Hierarchies

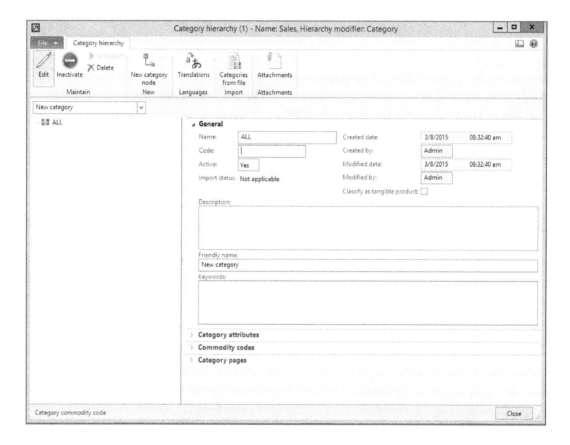

For the first level of the hierarchy set the **Name** to **ALL**.

Configuring Category Hierarchies

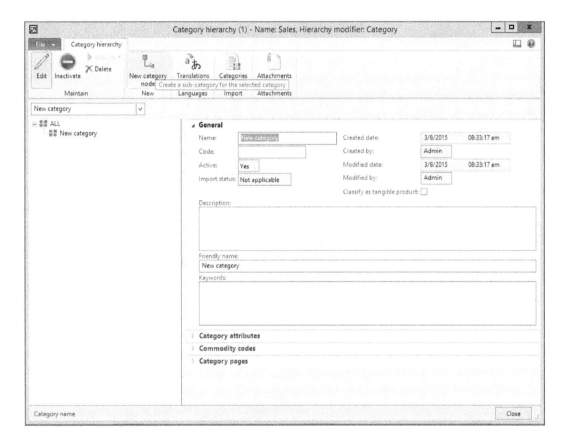

Then click on the **New Category Node** within the **New** group of the **Category Hierarchy** ribbon bar to create a child caregory.

Configuring Category Hierarchies

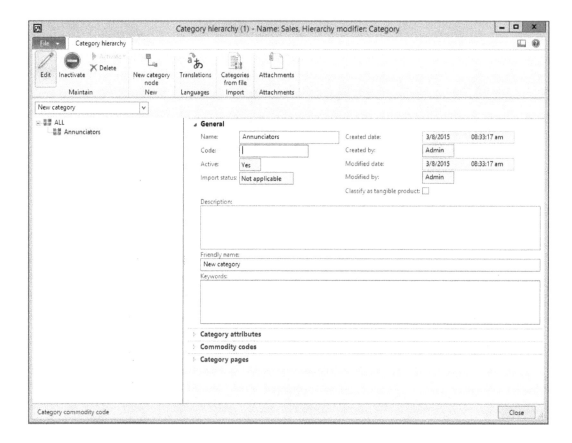

Set the **Name** to **Annunciators**.

Configuring Category Hierarchies

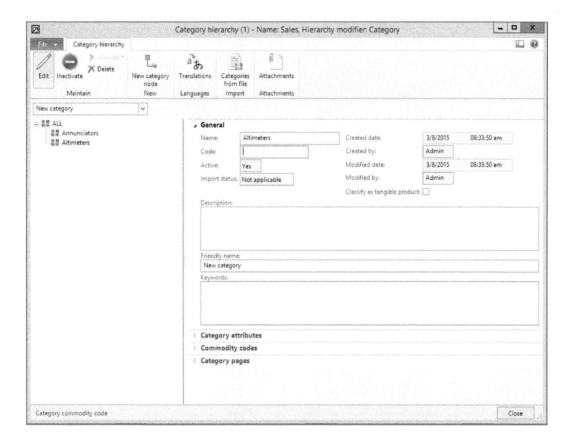

Keep on adding additional **Categories** to the **Category Hierarchy** and when you are done, click on the **Close** button to exit from the form.

Configuring Category Hierarchy Types

Category Hierarchies can be used in a number of different ways within Dynamics AX, including Sales, Purchasing, and even Financial hierarchies, so there is one last step in the setup of the **Category Hierarchies**, and that is to create and assign it to the right **Category Hierarchy Type**.

Configuring Category Hierarchy Types

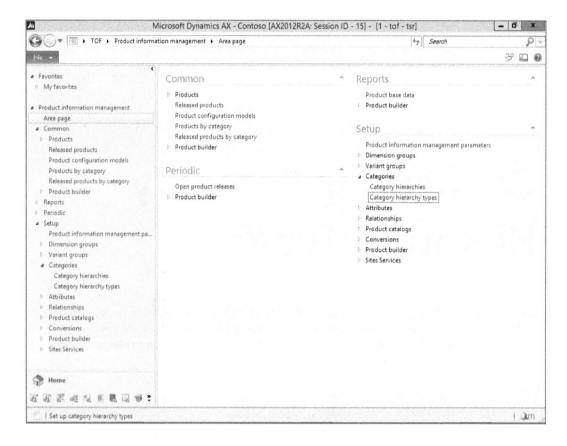

To do this, click on the **Category Hierarchy Types** menu item within the **Categories** folder of the **Setup** group within the **Product Information Management** area page.

Configuring Category Hierarchy Types

When the **Category Hierarchy Types** maintenance form is displayed, click on the **New** button in the menu bar to create a new record.

Configuring Category Hierarchy Types

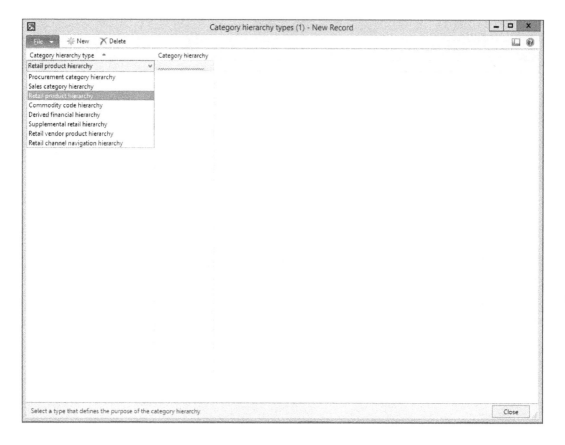

Then click on the dropdown list for the **Category Hierarchy Type** field to see all of the different options, and select the **Retail Product Hierarchy** record.

Configuring Category Hierarchy Types

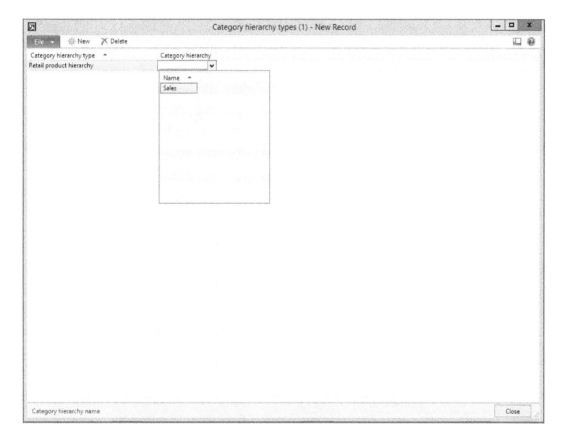

Then click on the dropdown list for the **Category Hierarchy** and select the **Sales Category Hierarchy** that you just created.

Configuring Category Hierarchy Types

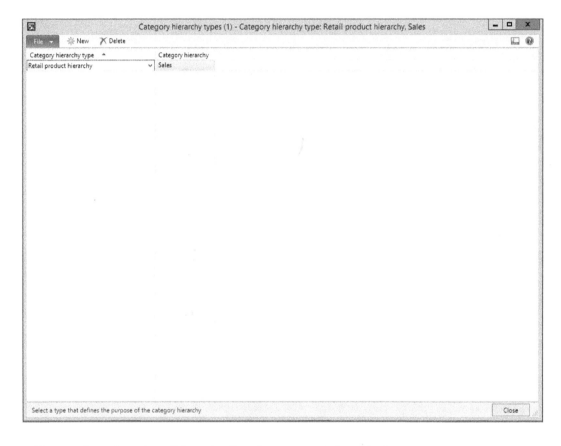

After you have done that click on the **Close** button to exit from the form.

Configuring Retail Category Attribute Groups

Now we can start configuring our default **Attributes** against our **Categories**. There is a trick to this though, because based off the **Category Hierarchy Type** that you have assigned to your **Category Hierarchy** you will have different options available to you and you will also need to maintain it within different areas. In this case we need to jump over to the **Retail** area to set up some data.

Configuring Retail Category Attribute Groups

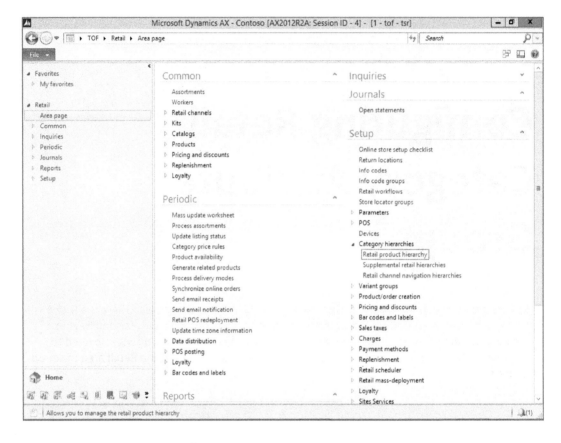

To do this click on the **Retail Product Hierarchy** menu item within the **Category Hierarchies** folder of the **Setup** group within the **Retail** area page.

Configuring Retail Category Attribute Groups

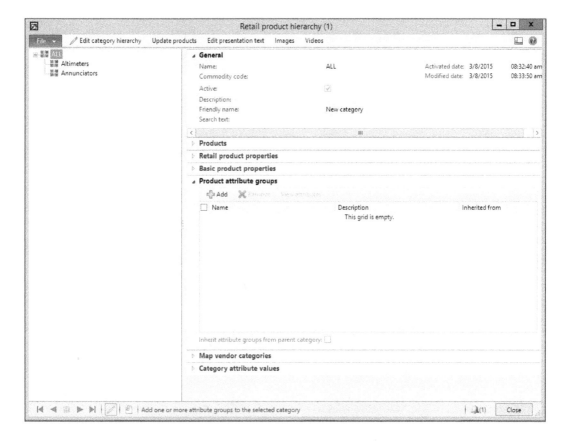

This will open up your **Category Hierarchy** that you just configured.

Configuring Retail Category Attribute Groups

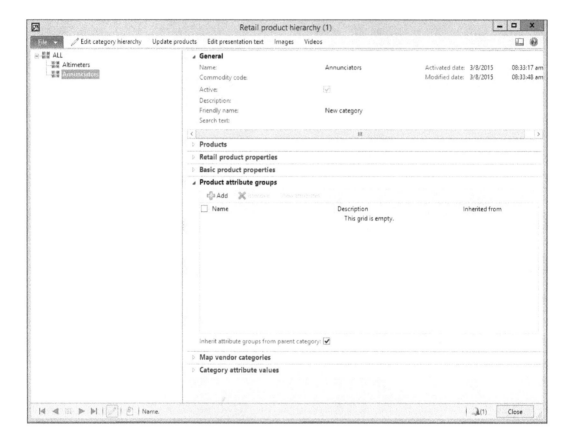

Select the **Annunciators** category, and then expand out the **Product Attribute Groups** tab group. Then click on the **Add** button.

Configuring Retail Category Attribute Groups

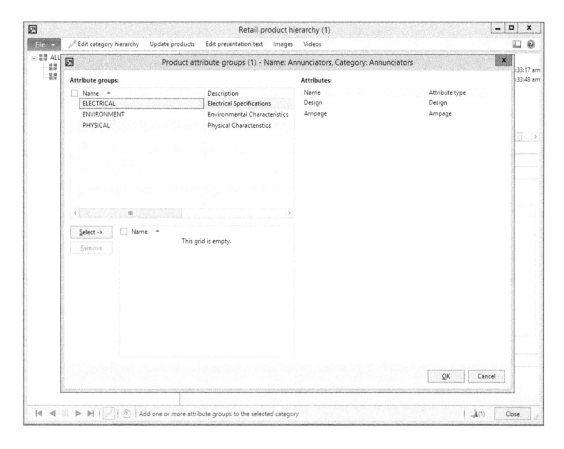

This will open up a selection dialog showing all of the **Product Attribute Groups** that you have configured.

Configuring Retail Category Attribute Groups

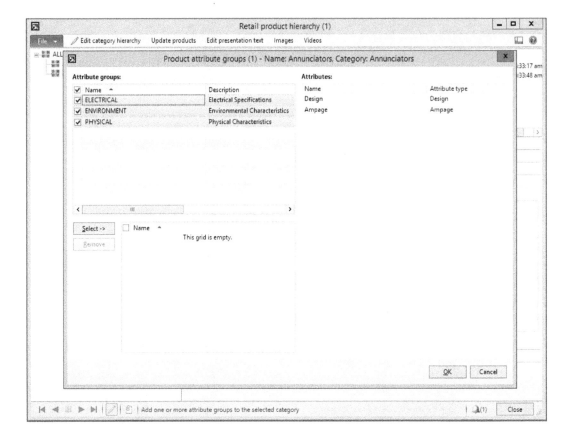

Select the **Attribute Groups** that you want to add to the **Category** and click on the **Select** button.

Configuring Retail Category Attribute Groups

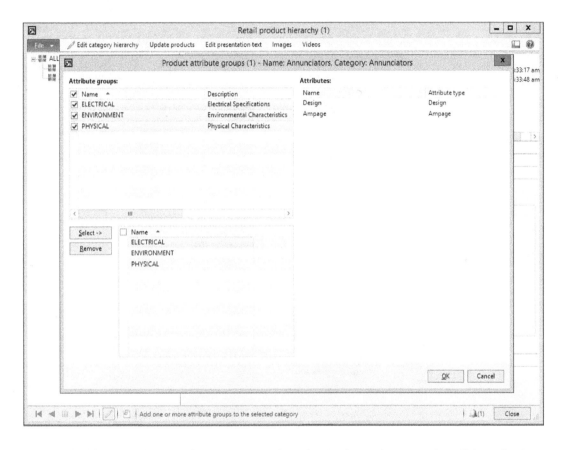

This will add the **Product Attribute Groups** to the selection list and you can then click on the **OK** button to exit from the form.

Configuring Retail Category Attribute Groups

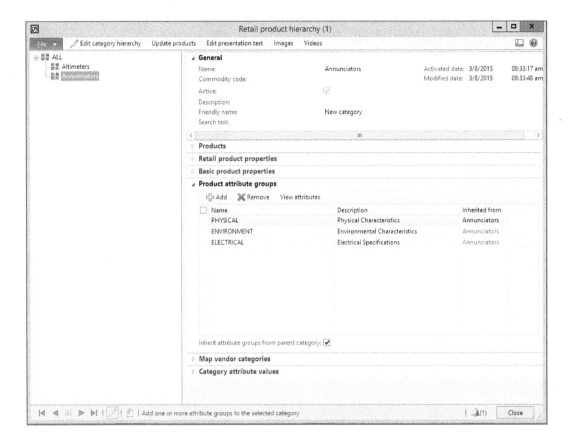

When you return back to the **Retail Product Hierarchies** maintenance form you will see that they have been added.

Associating Products With Product Categories

Now we can perform the last part of the setup, and that is to assign your products to their **Category** in the hierarchy, which will then link them with the **Attributes** that you have set up.

341

Associating Products With Product Categories

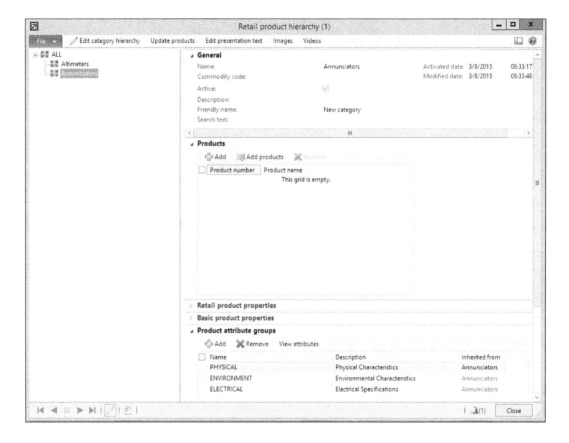

To do this return to the **Retail Product Hierarchy** maintenance form and expand out the **Products** tab group. Then click on the **Add** button in the menu bar for that tab.

Associating Products With Product Categories

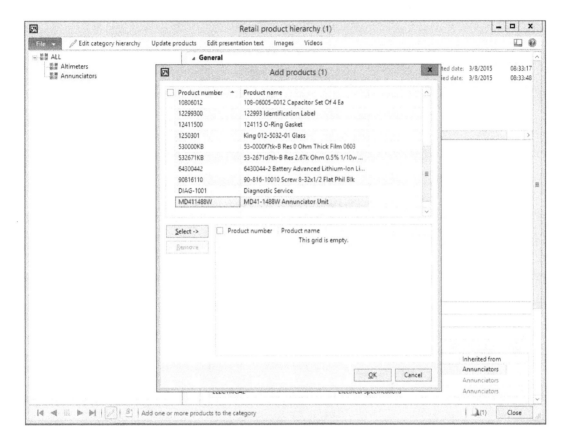

This will open up a list of all of the products that you have set up, and you can select the **MD411488W** product and click on the **Select** button.

Associating Products With Product Categories

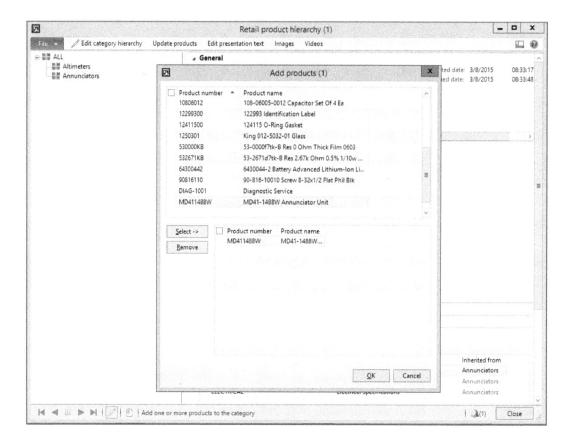

You can repeat the process and add as many other products that you like and when you are done, click on the **OK** button.

Associating Products With Product Categories

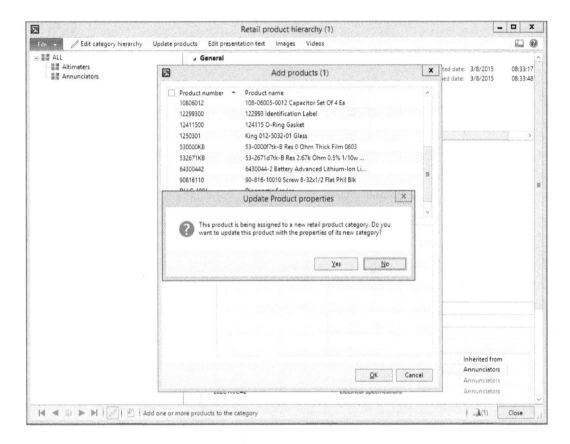

A dialog box will be displayed asking you if you want to update the product details with the defaults from the **Product Category**, and just click the **Yes** button.

Associating Products With Product Categories

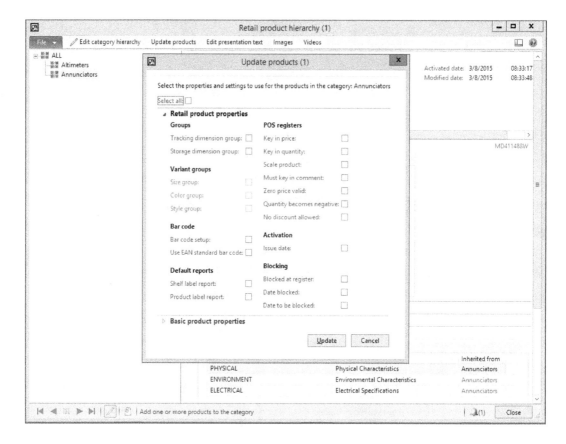

This will open up a dialog box that shows you all of the default information that you can copy from the **Category** to the **Product**.

Don't select any right now, and just click on the **Update** button.

Note: This is a great way to keep the product details consistent though.

Associating Products With Product Categories

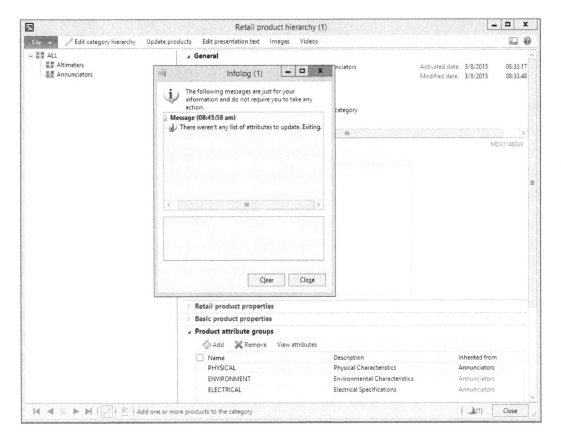

After you have done that you will get an InfoLog that says either that you have or have not updated some of the information, and you can click on the **Close** button and then close out of the **Retail Product Hierarchy** maintenance form.

Maintaining Product Attributes

Now we have all of the **Categories** and **Attributes** configured and associated with our products we can start setting up our **Product Attributes.**

Maintaining Product Attributes

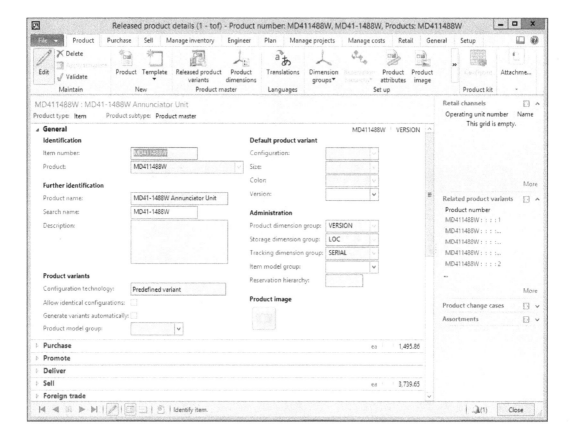

To do this open up the **Released Product Details** for the **MD411488W** product and then click on the **Product Attributes** button within the **Setup** group of the **Product** ribbon bar.

Maintaining Product Attributes

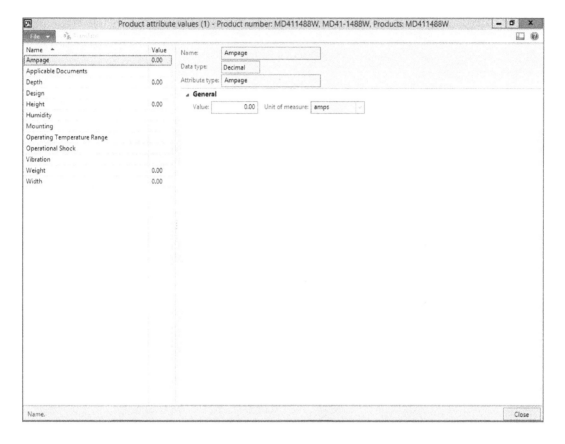

This will open up a maintenance form that shows you all of the **Attributes** that are associated with the product.

Maintaining Product Attributes

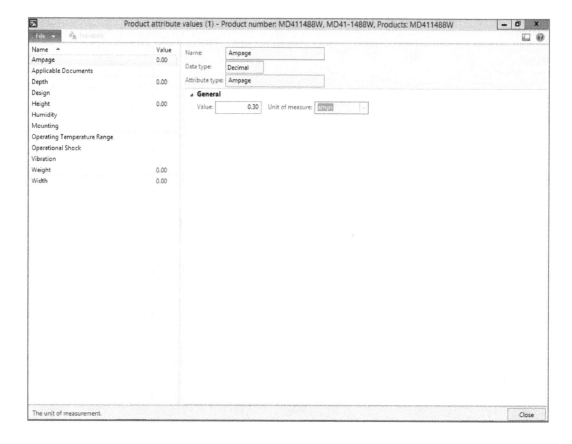

Select the **Ampage** attribute and change the **Value** to **0.30**.

Maintaining Product Attributes

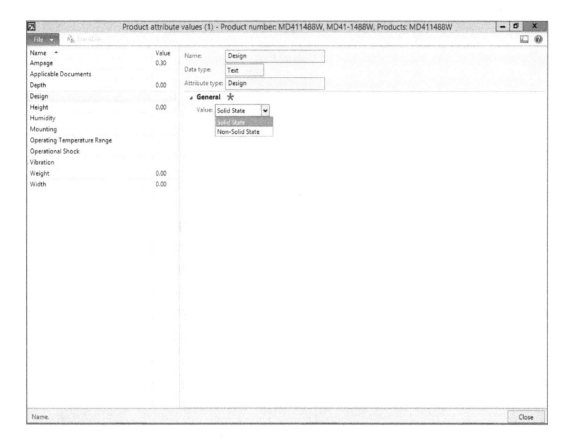

If you select the **Design** attribute then you will notice that you can only select between the two valid values that you defined.

Maintaining Product Attributes

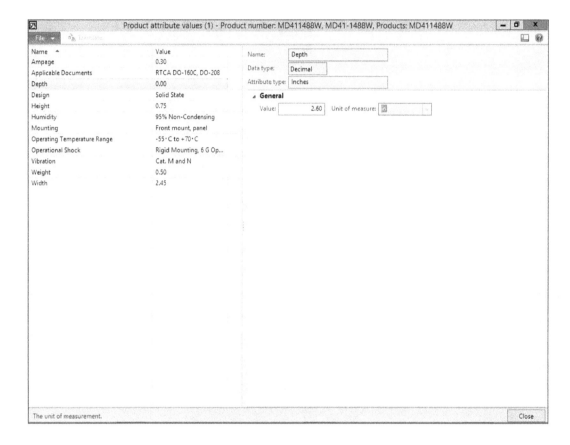

Now work through all of the **Attributes** and set their values.

When you are done, just click on the **Close** button to exit from the form.

CONFIGURING PRODUCT CATALOGS

Another useful feature that you can configure within Dynamics AX are the **Product Catalogs**. These have two important uses, the first is that is allows you to create product hierarchies that you can use within the **Customer Self Service Portal** shopping cart for customers that are browsing through the products, and the second is that you can set up additional descriptions and product images for your products that are more customer facing, including rich and HTML formatting.

357

Configuring Product Catalog Groups

First we will need to configure some **Product Catalog Groups**. These will be used to group products and also allows you to create a different type of Product Hierarchy.

Configuring Product Catalog Groups

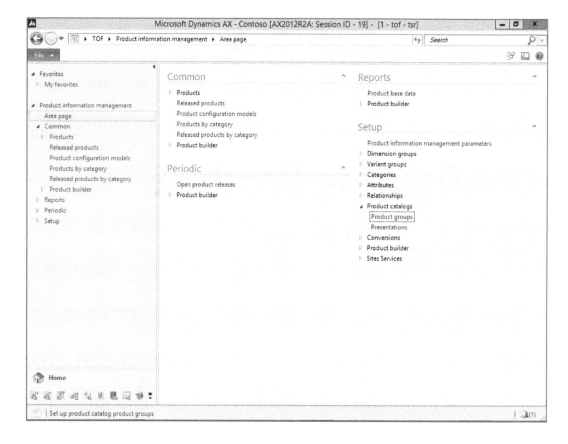

To do this, click on the **Product Groups** menu item within the **Product Catalogs** folder of the **Setup** group within the **Product Information Management** area page.

Configuring Product Catalog Groups

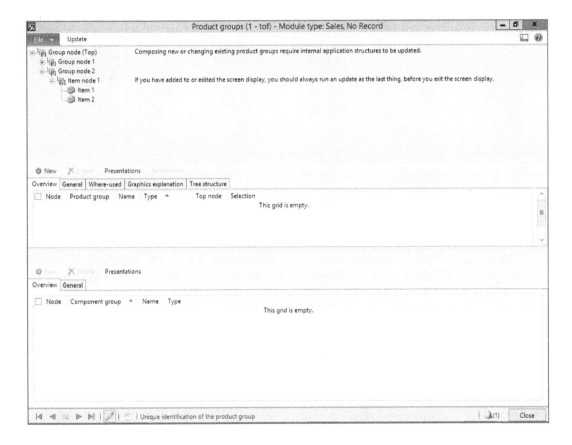

This will open up the **Product Groups** maintenance form which will allow us to create our hierarchy tree.

Configuring Product Catalog Groups

To start off, click on the **New** button within the menu bar to create your first record.

Configuring Product Catalog Groups

First we will create a **Product** Group that will contain all of our group products. To do this set the **Product Group** and **Name** to **Annunciators**, and then click on the **Type** dropdown list and select **Item Node** value.

Configuring Product Catalog Groups

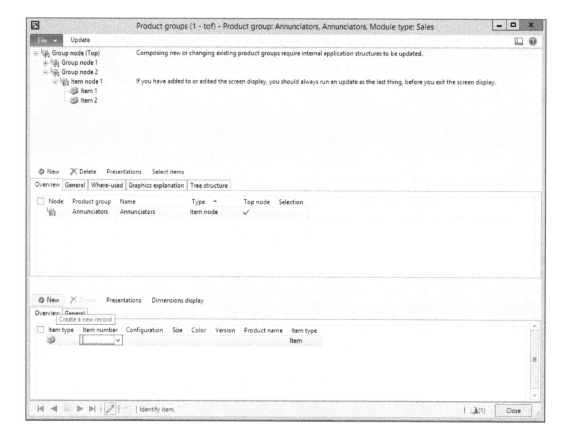

Then click on the **New** button in the lower form to create a new child record.

Configuring Product Catalog Groups

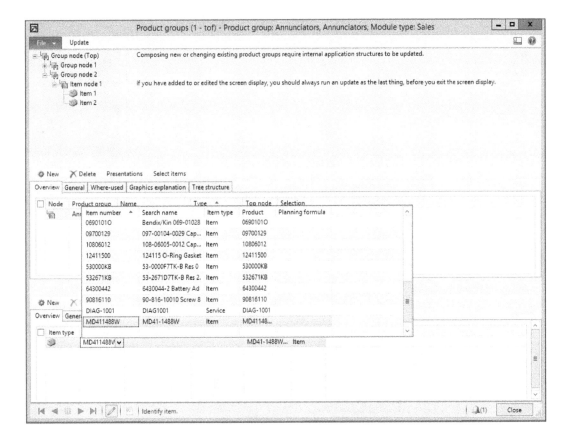

Click on the **Item Number** dropdown list, and since this is an **Item Node** you will be able to select the **MD411488W** product from the dropdown list.

Configuring Product Catalog Groups

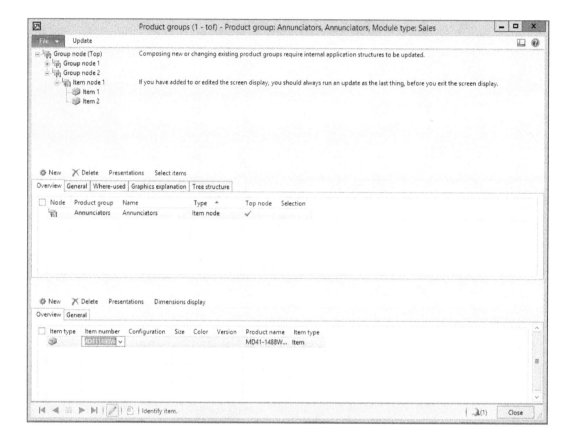

That will default in the product name etc.

Configuring Product Catalog Groups

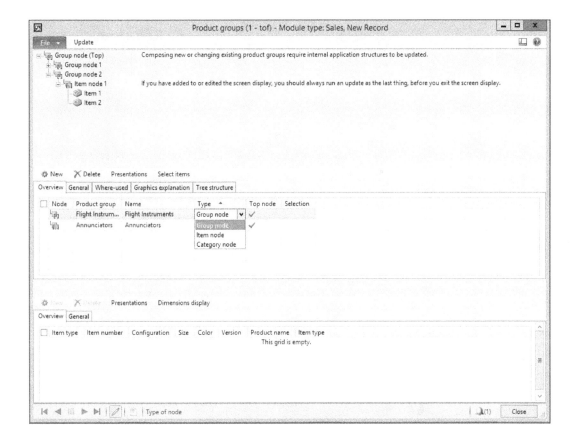

Now we will create a parent category that will include the **Item Node**. To do this, click on the **New** button in the menu bar to create a new record. Then set the **Product Group** and **Name** to **Flight Instruments** and set the **Type** to **Group Node**.

Configuring Product Catalog Groups

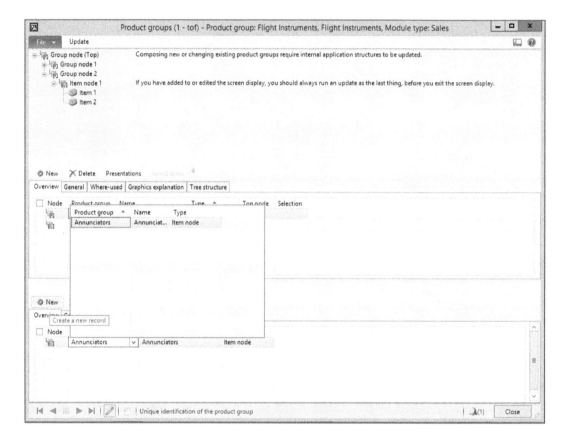

Then click on the **New** button in the footer table to create a new child record and when you click on the **Component Group** dropdown list you will be able to select the **Annunciators Item Group** that you just created.

Configuring Product Catalog Groups

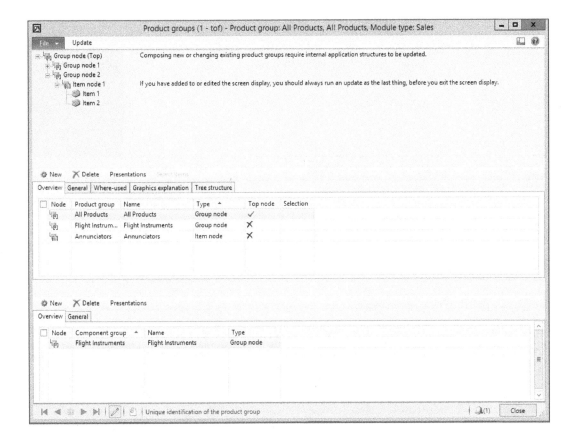

Click on the **New** button in the menu bar again to create another record, and set the **Product Group** and **Name** to **All Products**, the **Type** to **Group Node** and then assign the **Flight Instruments** as a child node.

Configuring Product Catalog Groups

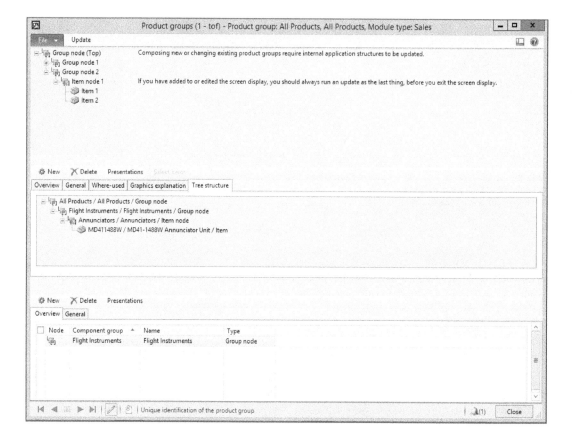

If you select the **Tree Structure** tab you will see the complete hierarchy including the products.

You can keep on building out the categories and when you are done, click on the **Close** button to exit from the form.

Configuring Product Presentation Details

Once you have the **Product Catalog Hierarchies** defined then you can start to use them to track some of the other presentation based content that is more customer facing.

Configuring Product Presentation Details

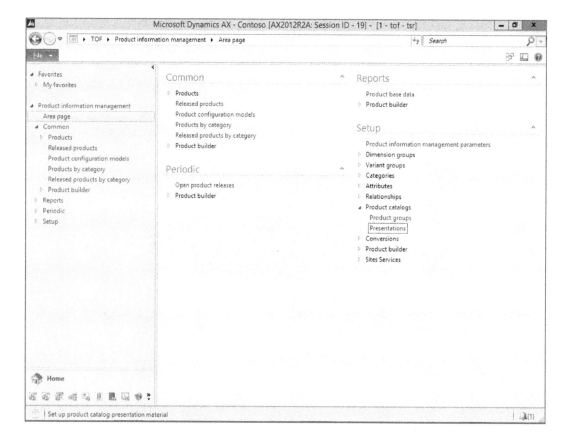

To do this, click on the **Presentations** menu item within the **Product Catalogs** folder of the **Setup** group within the **Product Information Management** area page.

Configuring Product Presentation Details

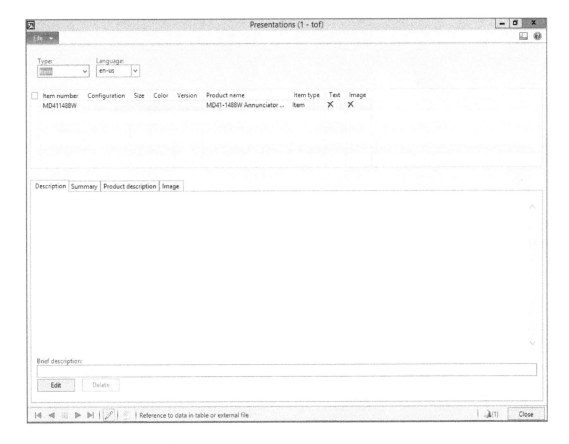

This will open up a list of all the products that you have defined within your **Product Catalog**. Select the **MD411488W** product and click the **Edit** button below the **Description**.

Configuring Product Presentation Details

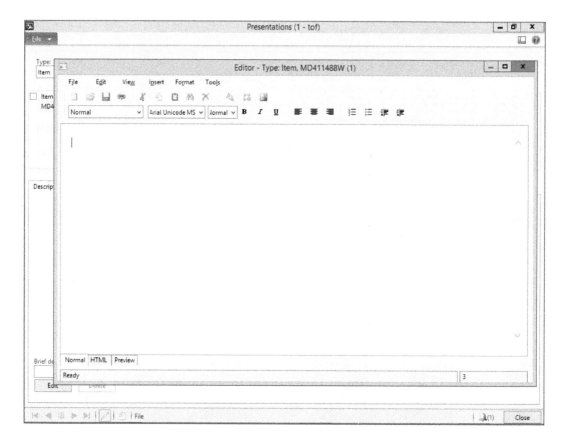

This will open up a rich text editor that you can then use to add a better product description.

Configuring Product Presentation Details

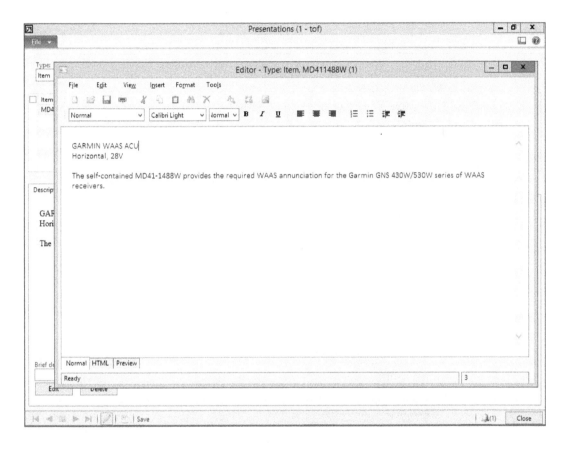

Just type in (or cut and paste in) your product description, click on the save icon in the menu bar, and then close out of the editor.

Configuring Product Presentation Details

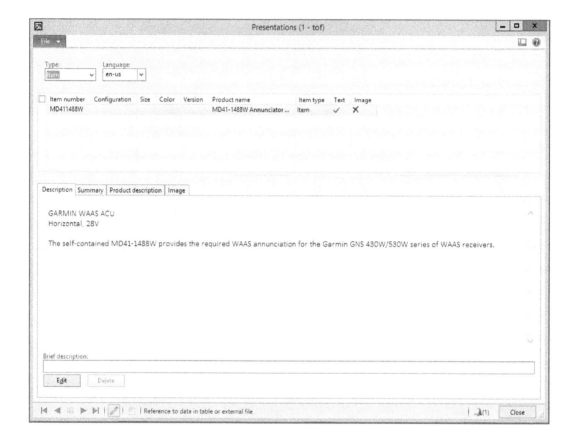

Now you will see the prettier description.

Configuring Product Presentation Details

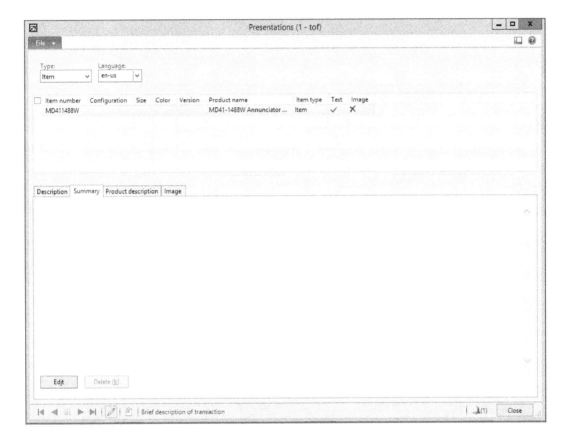

You can also add a summary description for your product by switching to the **Summary** tab and clicking on the **Edit** button.

Configuring Product Presentation Details

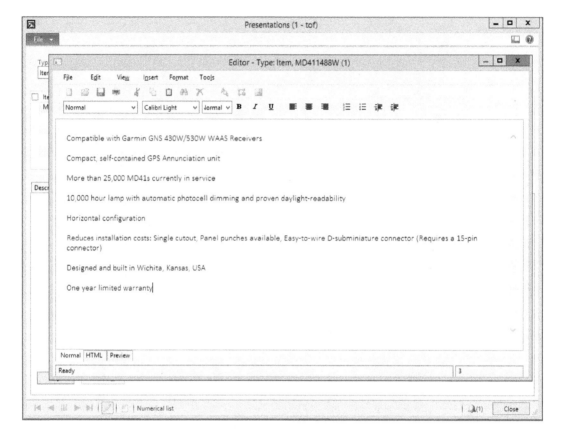

When the rich text editor is displayed, cut and paste in the summary details and then save and close out of the editor.

Configuring Product Presentation Details

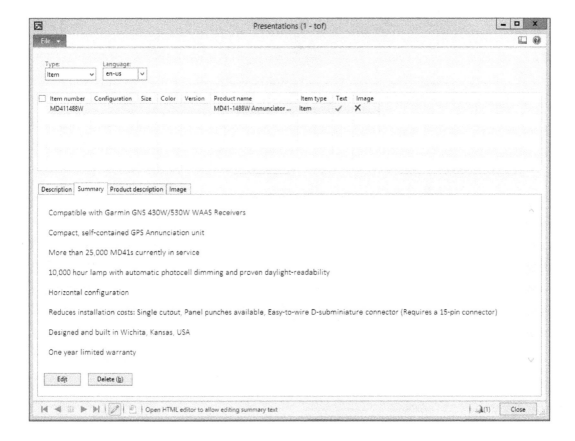

Now you have summary information.

Configuring Product Presentation Details

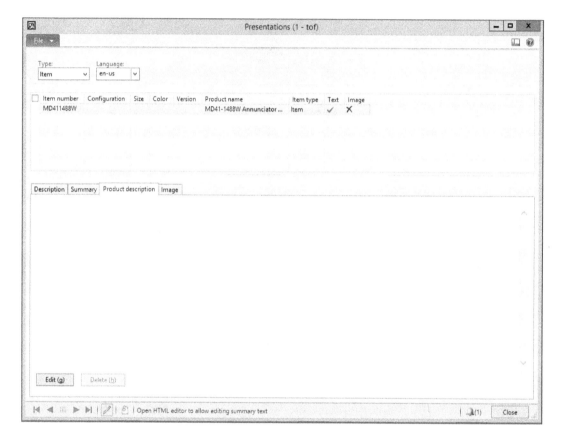

Now switch to the **Product Description** tab and click on the **Edit** button.

Configuring Product Presentation Details

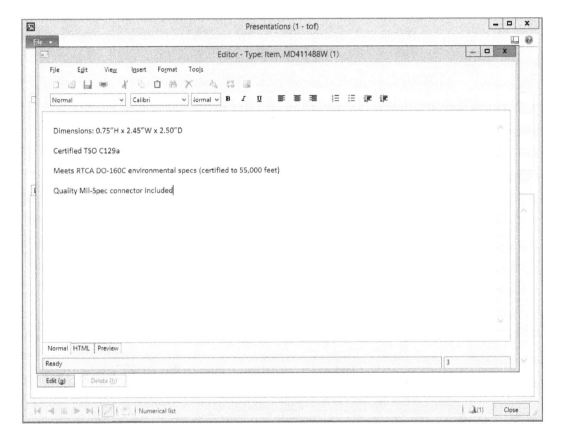

Cut and paste in the **Product Description** and then save and close out of the form.

Configuring Product Presentation Details

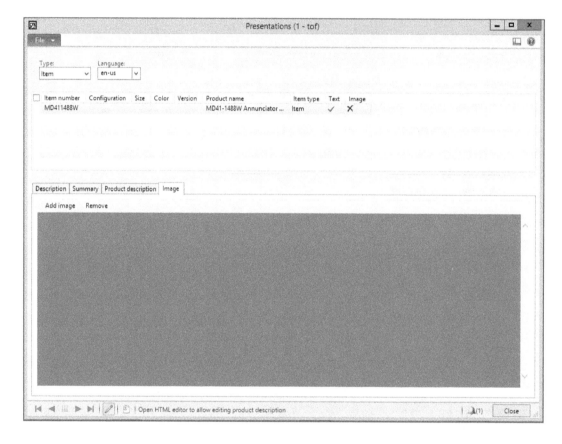

The final piece of presentation information that you can configure are the **Product Images**. To do this, select the **Image** tab and then click on the **Add Image** link button in the header.

Configuring Product Presentation Details

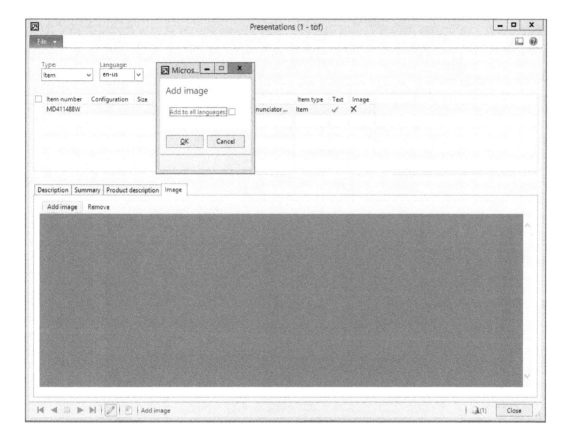

A dialog box will be displayed asking you if you want to use the same image for all languages. If you do, then check the **Add To All Languages** flag and then click on the **OK** button.

Configuring Product Presentation Details

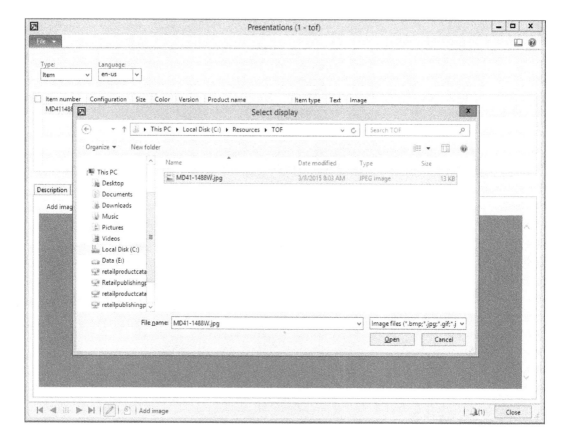

Then a file explorer window will be displayed and you will be able to navigate to where you have your product image stored, select it and then click on the **Open** button.

Configuring Product Presentation Details

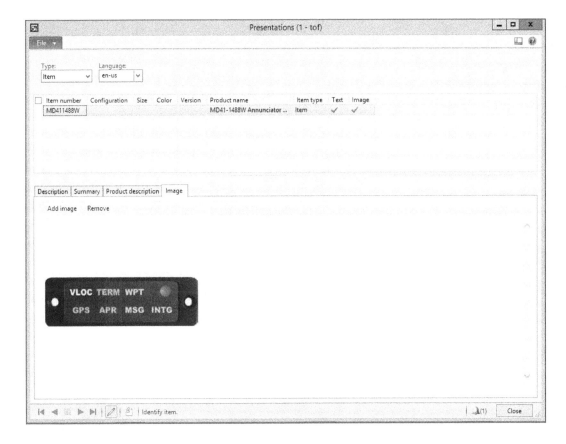

When you return back to the **Presentation** form you will see a picture of the product.

Configuring Product Group Presentation Details

The presentation information is not just related to the **Products** though, you can also set up default descriptions and images for the group nodes.

Configuring Product Group Presentation Details

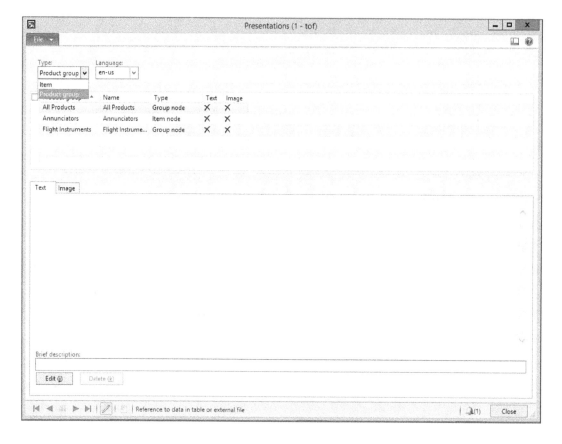

To do this click on the **Type** dropdown list within the **Presentations** form and select the **Product Group** value.

daxc

Configuring Product Group Presentation Details

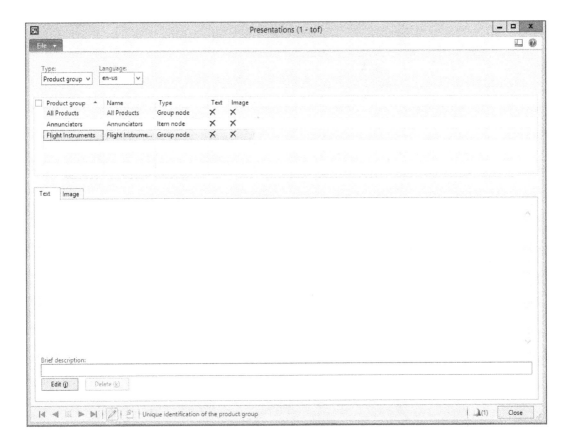

This will change the list from showing products to product groups. Select the **Flight Instruments Product Group** and click on the **Edit** button below the **Text** field.

Configuring Product Group Presentation Details

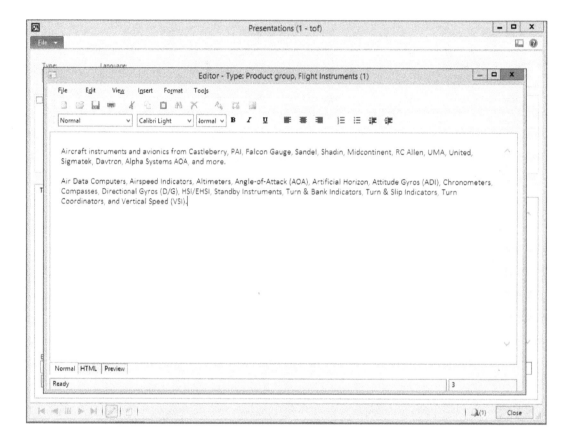

This will open up the editor and you can type in (or cut and paste in) the description for that product group. When you are done, save the text and then close out of the form.

Configuring Product Group Presentation Details

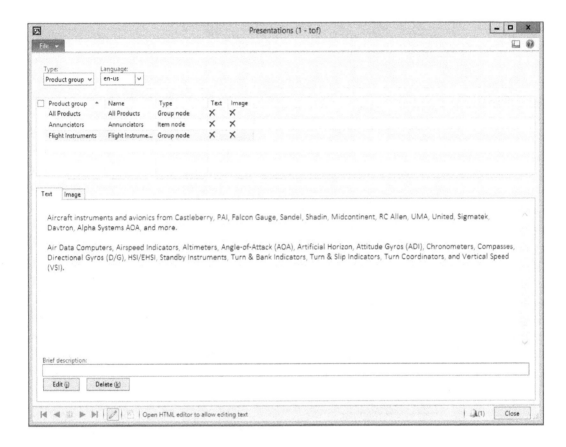

Now you will be able to see the text description for the node.

Configuring Product Group Presentation Details

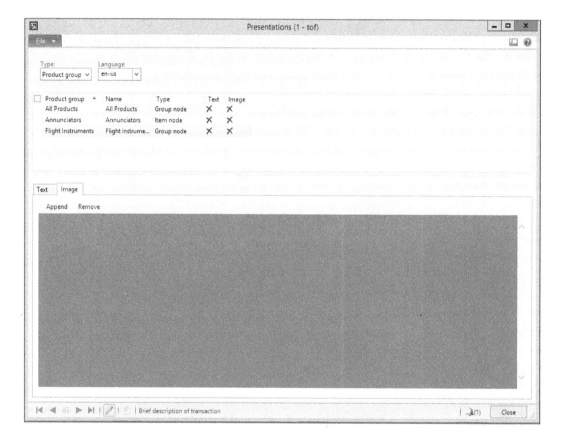

You can also add pictures to the product groups as well. To do this, switch to the **Image** tab and click on the **Append** button.

Configuring Product Group Presentation Details

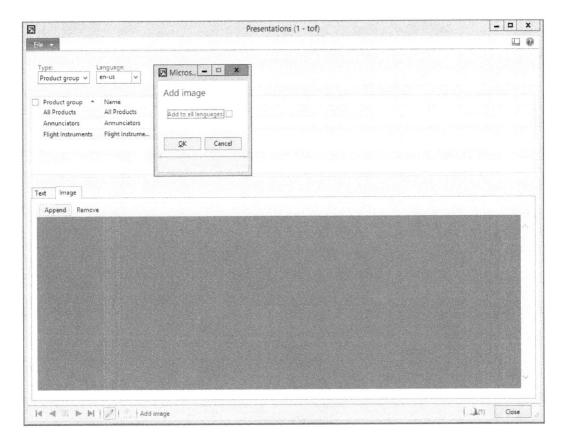

A dialog box will be displayed asking you if you want to use the same image for all languages. If you do, then check the **Add To All Languages** flag and then click on the **OK** button.

Configuring Product Group Presentation Details

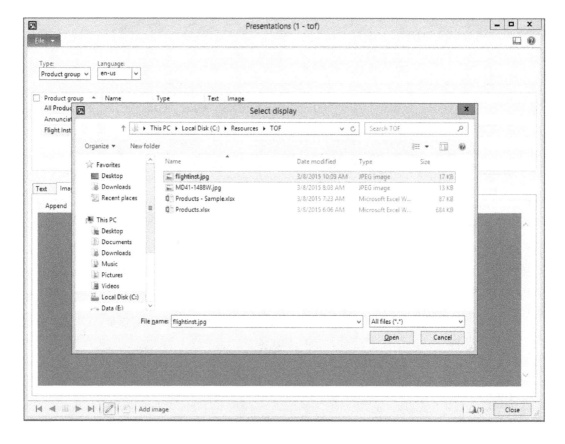

Then a file explorer window will be displayed and you will be able to navigate to where you have your product group image stored, select it and then click on the **Open** button.

Configuring Product Group Presentation Details

Now you will have a product group image.

How cool is that.

After you have updated all of the groups, click on the **Close** button to exit from the form.

CONFIGURING PRODUCT RELATIONSHIPS

Another feature within the Product Information Management area that you may want to configure is the **Product Relationships** function. This allows you to create links between products to indicate that products are sold together, are alternate products, are commonly purchased together, or really anything that you like.

Configuring Product Relationship Types

The first step is to set up the different **Product Relationship Types** that you want to track.

Configuring Product Relationship Types

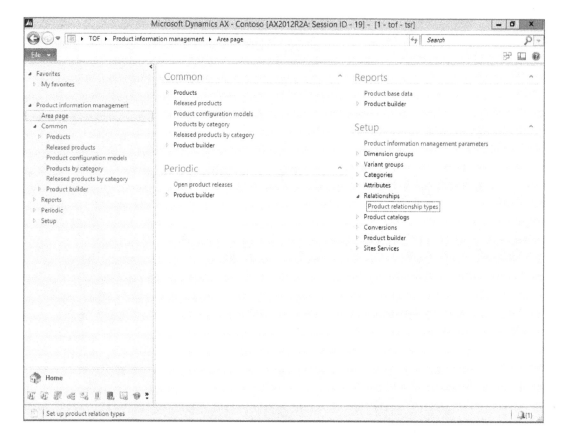

To do this, click on the **Product Relationship Types** menu item within the **Relationships** folder of the **Setup** group within the **Product Information Management** area page.

Configuring Product Relationship Types

When the **Product Relationship Types** maintenance form is displayed, click on the **New** button within the menu bar to create a new record.

Configuring Product Relationship Types

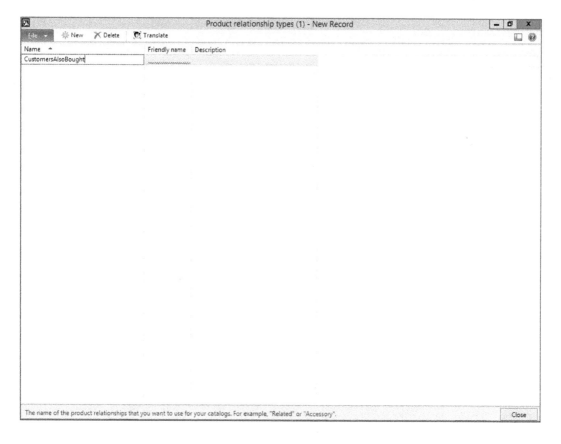

Set the **Name** to **CustomerAlsoBought**.

Configuring Product Relationship Types

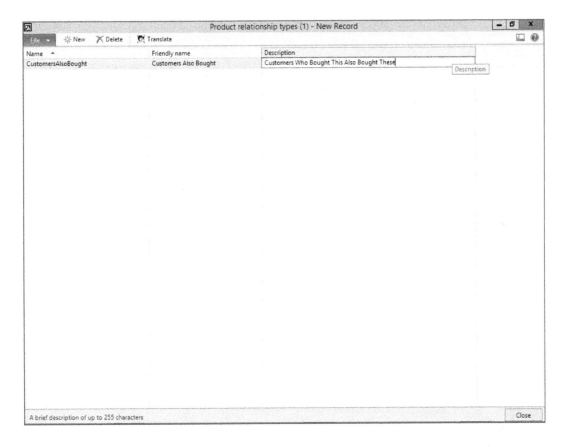

Then set the **Friendly Name** to **Customer Also Bought** and the **Description** to **Customers Who Bought This Also Bought These.**

Configuring Product Relationship Types

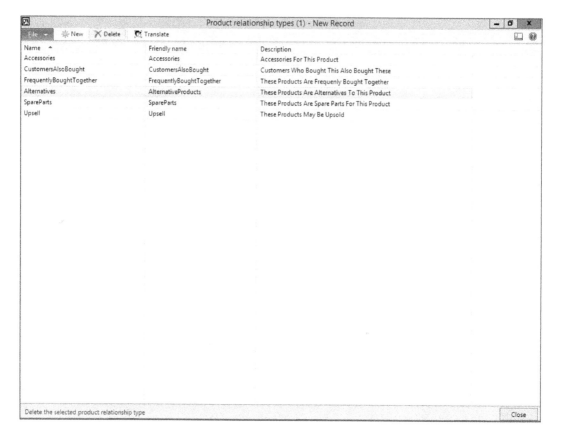

Repeat the process for all of the other types of relationships that you want to track and then click on the **Close** button to exit from the form.

Configuring Product Relationships

Once you have defined the **Relationships** you can start using them within the **Released Products**.

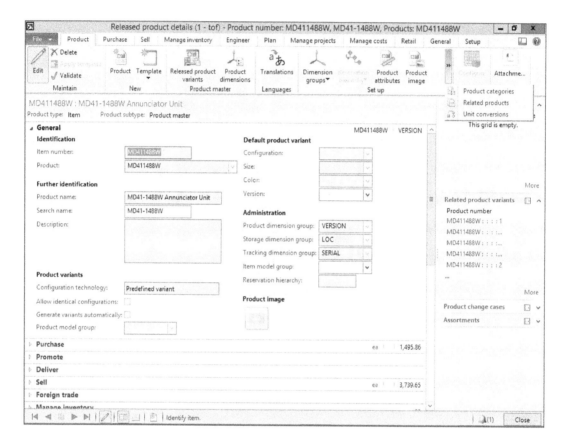

To do this, open up the **Released Product Details** form, and click on the **Related Products** menu item within the **Setup** group of the **Products** ribbon bar.

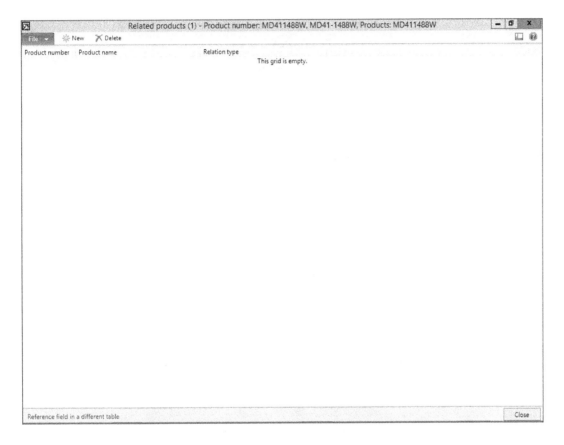

This will open up the **Related Products** maintenance form. Click on the **New** button in the menu bar to create a new record.

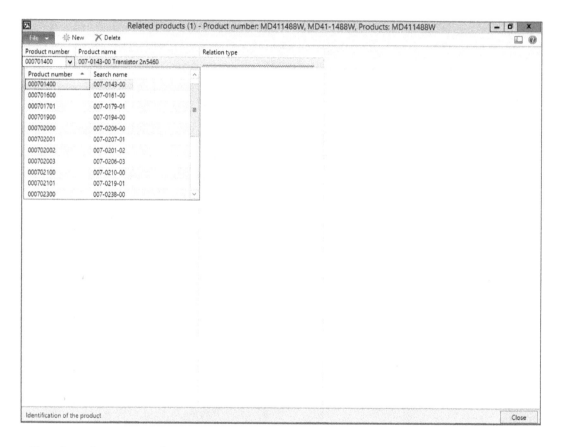

Then from the **Item Number** dropdown list select a product.

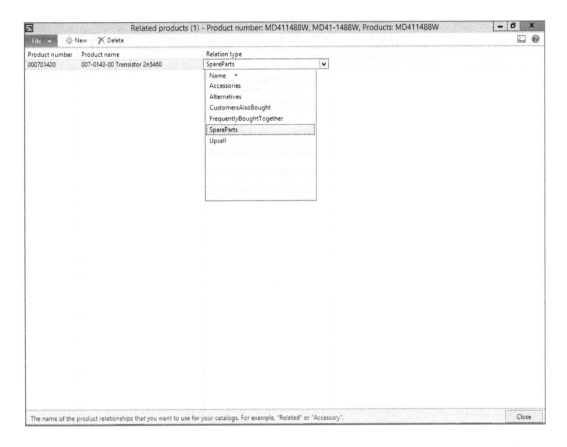

Then click on the **Relationship Type** dropdown list select the type of relationship that links the two products – in this case we will use **SpareParts** to indicate that this is a spare part for the parent item.

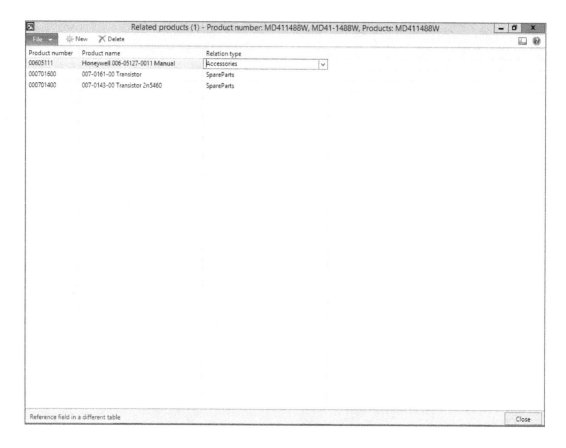

You can keep on adding as many different relationships as you like, and then when you are done, click on the **Close** button to exit from the form.

CONFIGURING PRODUCT CHANGE MANAGEMENT CASES

If you make changes to your products periodically based on requests, or if you want to add more control to your product change management process, then you can do this within Dynamics AX by configuring **Product Change Management Cases**. These allow you to make change requests and then track the change statuses.

Creating A Product Change Case Category

To enable this feature you just need to create a **Case Category** for your product change requests.

Creating A Product Change Case Category

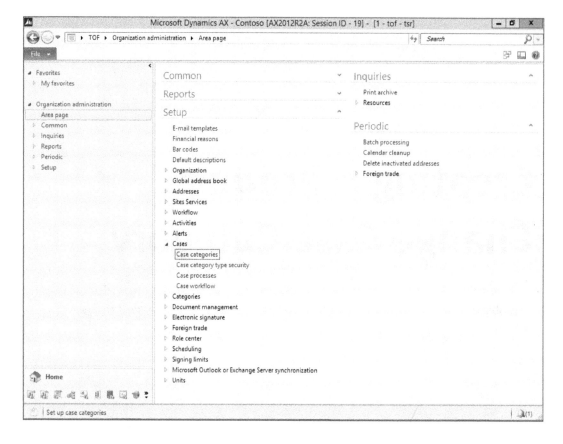

To do this, click on the **Case Categories** menu item within the **Cases** folder of the **Setup** group within the **Organization Administration** area page.

Creating A Product Change Case Category

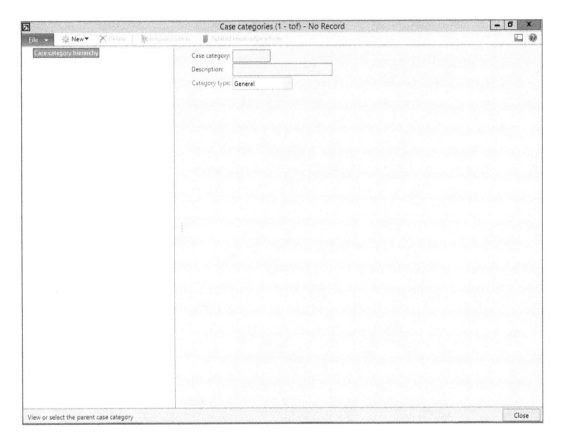

This will open up the **Case Categories** maintenance form.

Creating A Product Change Case Category

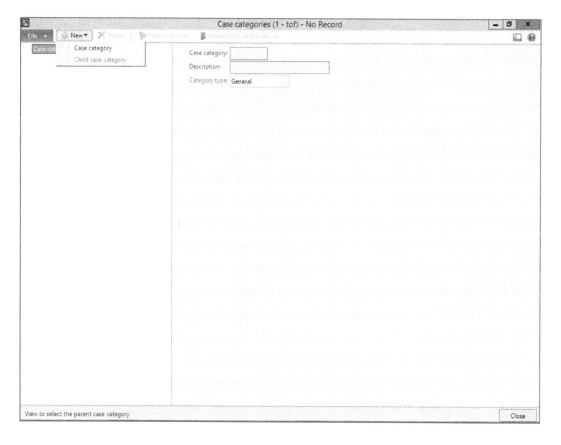

Click on the **New** button in the menu bar and select the **Case Category** submenu item.

Creating A Product Change Case Category

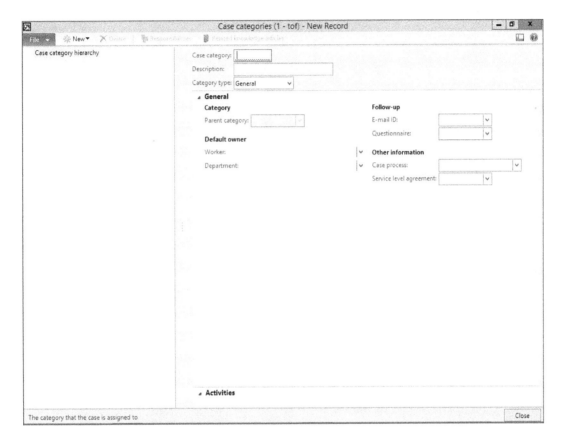

This will create a new **Case Category** record for you.

Creating A Product Change Case Category

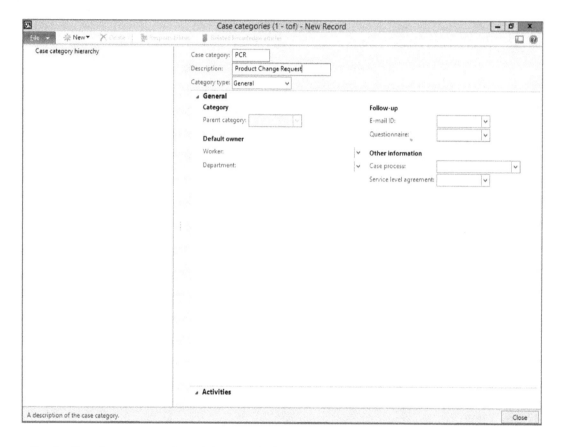

Set the **Case Category** to **PCR** and the **Description** to **Product Change Request**.

Creating A Product Change Case Category

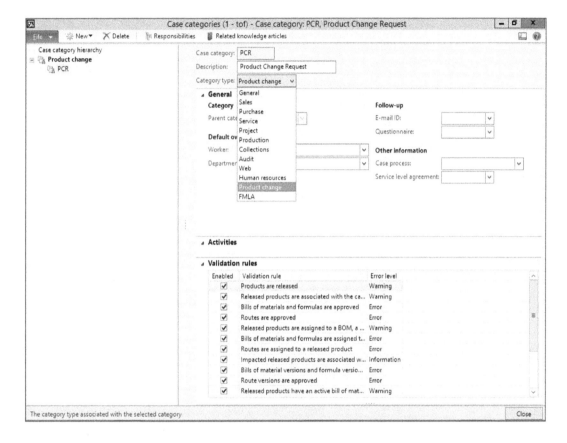

Then click on the **Category Type** and select the **Product Change** option.

Creating A Product Change Case Category

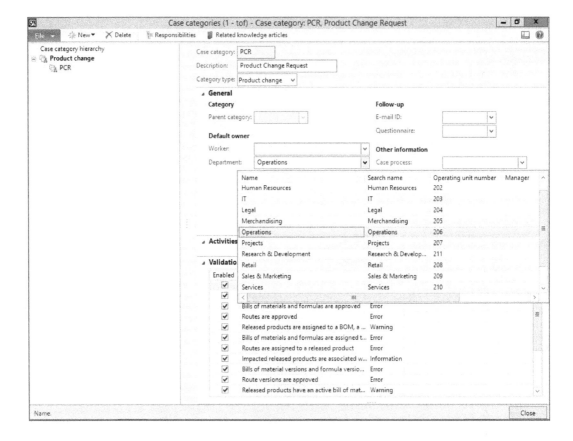

If you want you can have all of these cases assigned to a specific department by clicking on the **Department** dropdown list and selecting the **Operations** department.

Creating A Product Change Case Category

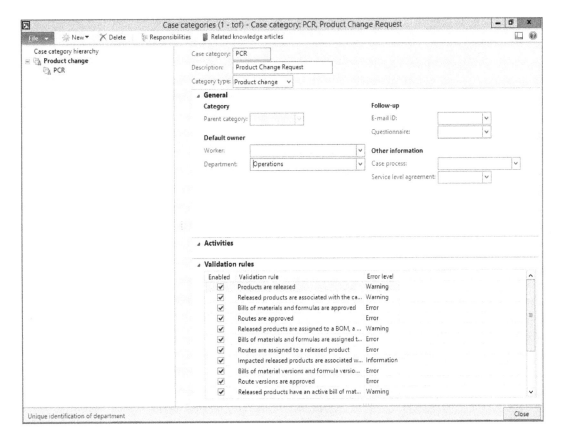

Once you have done this you can just click on the **Close** button and exit from the form.

Creating A Product Change Request Case

Now that you have a **Product Change Request** case type you can use it to request changes on products.

Creating A Product Change Request Case

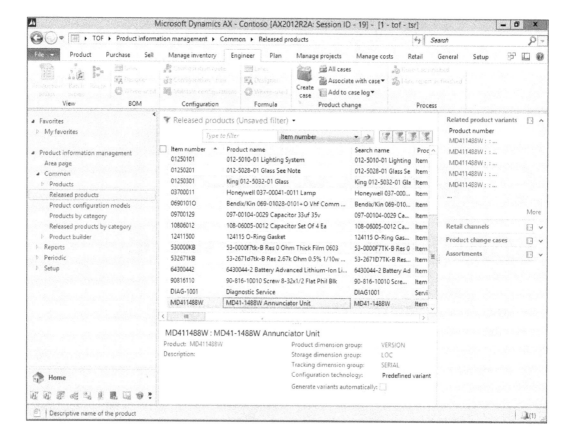

To do this, Open up your **Released Products** list form and select the **MD411488W** product and then click on the **Create Case** button within the **Product Change** group of the **Engineer** ribbon bar.

Creating A Product Change Request Case

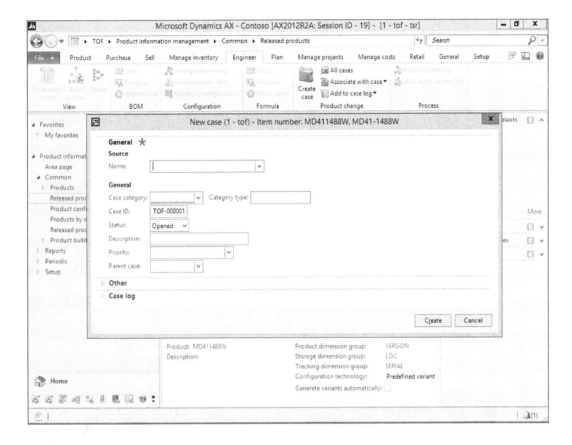

That will open up a **New Case** dialog box.

Creating A Product Change Request Case

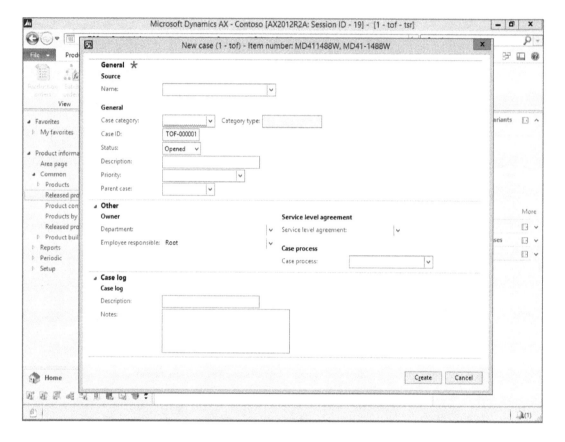

If you expand out all of the tab groups then you will see that there is more detail that you can enter if you like.

Creating A Product Change Request Case

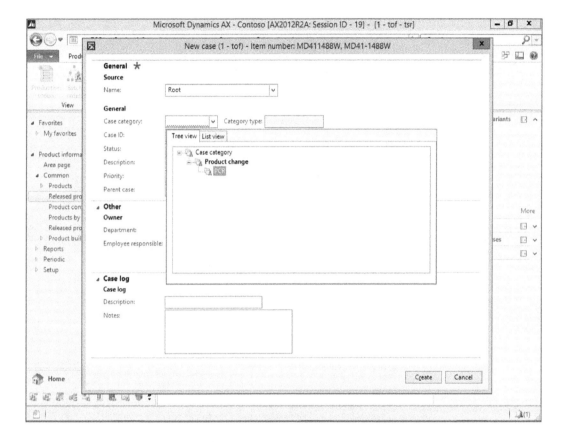

Click on the **Case Category** dropdown list and you will be able to choose your Product Change case that you just created.

DYNAMICS AX BARE BONES CONFIGURATION GUIDES
CONFIGURING PRODUCT INFORMATION MANAGEMENT WITHIN DYNAMICS AX 2012

Creating A Product Change Request Case

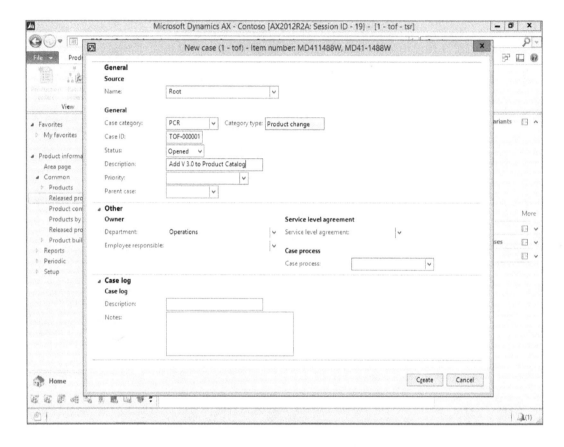

Then you can add a **Description** to the case.

© 2015 Blind Squirrel Publishing, LLC, All Rights Reserved
www.dynamicsaxcompanions.com

434

Creating A Product Change Request Case

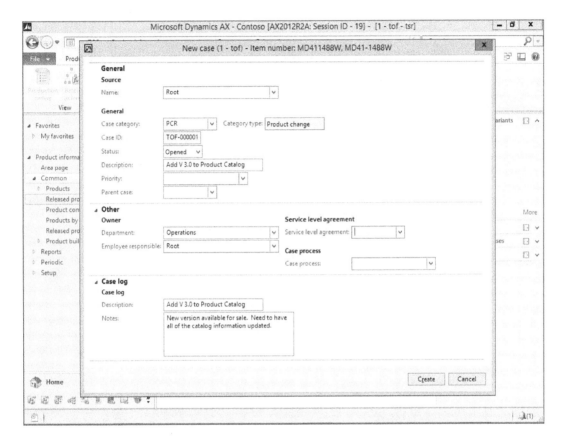

Note: If you defined a default **Department** for the case category then that well be defaulted in here.

If you want to add more detailed descriptions for the case then you can add more detail within the **Case Log** tab group, including **Descriptions** and also **Notes.**

When you are done, just click on the **Create** button to create the case.

Creating A Product Change Request Case

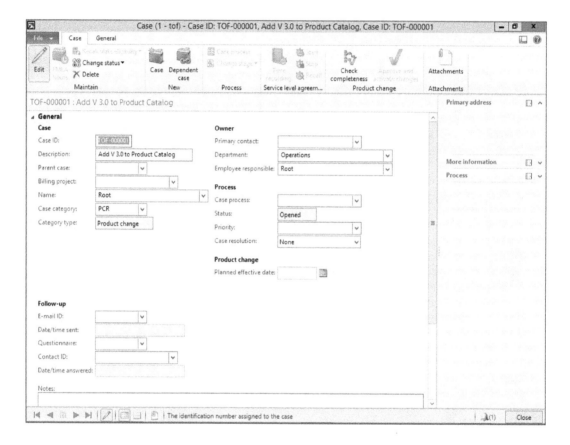

That will open up the full **Case** detail form and you can start fleshing out more of the details.

Creating A Product Change Request Case

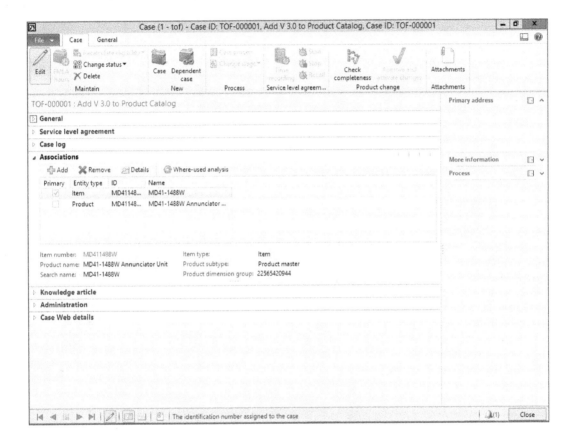

If you expand out the **Associations** tab group then you will also see that this case is linked to the product.

Now you have a way to track all product requests.

When you are done, click on the **Close** button to exit from the form.

SUMMARY

Hopefully this guide has given you a good foundation of knowledge of how the Product Information Management area of Dynamics AX works, and also some of the key features that are available for you that allow you to track and manage all of the product master records, to manage the external presentation information, and also a brief introduction into how you can start managing the product lifecycle within Dynamics AX.

We are still just scratching the surface with this guide though and there is so much more that you can do within the Product Information Management area. You can create models to configure and price your products, you can extend out the PLM case management to include processes and workflows, and you can start tracking the engineering details of the product.

So don't stop poking around in this area because there is still so much more that you can take advantage of.

Want More Tips & Tricks For Dynamics AX?

The Tips & Tricks series is a compilation of all the cool things that I have found that you can do within Dynamics AX, and are also the basis for my Tips & Tricks presentations that I have been giving for the AXUG, and online. Unfortunately book page size restrictions mean that I can only fit 50 tips & tricks per book, but I will create new volumes every time I reach the 50 Tip mark.

To get all of the details on this series, then here is the link:

http://dynamicsaxcompanions.com/tipsandtricks

Need More Help With Dynamics AX?

LUKE SKYWALKER MAY HAVE HAD THE FORCE,
BUT HE STILL NEEDED R2D2 TO PLOT THE
COURSE FOR HIM.
WHO IS YOUR COMPANION THAT WILL HELP YOU
NAVIGATE DYNAMICS AX?

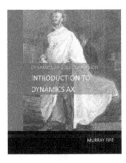

After creating a number of my walkthroughs on SlideShare showing how to configure the different areas within Dynamics AX, I had a lot of requests for the original documents so that people could get a better view of many of the screen shots and also have a easy reference as they worked through the same process within their own systems. To make them easier to access, I am in the process of moving all of the content to the Dynamics AX Companions website to easier access. If you are looking for details on how to configure and use Dynamics AX, then this is a great place for you to start.

Here is the link for the site:

http://dynamicsaxcompanions.com/

About Me

I am an author - I'm no Dan Brown but my books do contain a lot of secret codes and symbols that help guide you through the mysteries of Dynamics AX.

I am a curator - gathering all of the information that I can about Dynamics AX and filing it away within the Dynamics AX Companions archives.

I am a pitchman - I am forever extolling the virtues of Dynamics AX to the unwashed masses convincing them that it is the best ERP system in the world.

I am a Microsoft MVP - this is a big deal, there are less than 10 Dynamics AX MVP's in the US, and less than 30 worldwide.

I am a programmer - I know enough to get around within code, although I leave the hard stuff to the experts so save you all from my uncommented style.

WEB	www.murrayfife.me www.dynamicsaxcompanions.com
EMAIL	murray@dynamicsaxcompanions.com
TWITTER	@murrayfife
SKYPE	murrayfife
AMAZON	www.amazon.com/author/murrayfife

www.ingramcontent.com/pod-product-compliance
Lightning Source LLC
Chambersburg PA
CBHW080142060326
40689CB00018B/3825